GET THE LIFE YOU WANT

RICHARD BANDLER

Edited by Owen Fitzpatrick

HARPER
element

Harper*Element*
An Imprint of HarperCollins*Publishers*
77–85 Fulham Palace Road,
Hammersmith, London W6 8JB
www.harpercollins.co.uk

and Harper*Element* are trademarks of
HarperCollins*Publishers* Limited

Published by Harper*Element* 2008

4

A catalogue record of this book
is available from the British Library

ISBN 978-0-00-729251-6

Printed and bound in Great Britain by
Clays Ltd, St Ives plc

Mixed Sources
Product group from well-managed
forests and other controlled sources
www.fsc.org Cert no. SW-COC-1806
© 1996 Forest Stewardship Council

FSC

FSC is a non-profit international organisation established to promote the
responsible management of the world's forests. Products carrying the FSC
label are independently certified to assure consumers that they come
from forests that are managed to meet the social, economic and
ecological needs of present and future generations.

Find out more about HarperCollins and the environment at
www.harpercollins.co.uk/green

To John and Kathleen LaValle, the best friends I have ever had.
And to Dr Robert Spitzer for helping me to get started.

CONTENTS

Part 2: Getting Through It

Part 3: Getting To It

FOREWORD
by Paul McKenna

Years ago, a mobile phone was expensive to buy, difficult to use and the size of a small brick. Now there are phones that fit in the palm of your hand and you can not only use them to make calls but also to read e-mails, surf the net, and even watch TV.

In the same way, Richard Bandler's life work has transformed our understanding of the true capacity of the human mind. In my considered opinion, he is the greatest creative genius of personal change alive today.

As proof, you need look no further than Neuro-Linguistic Programming, the field he developed almost 40 years ago. Once on the fringes of conventional psychology, NLP is now studied, taught and practiced all over the planet.

For example, trained professional psychologists used to struggle to remove a patient's phobia over a 6 month period. Now, by simply applying the techniques Richard has developed, most phobias can be completely eliminated in less than an hour and smaller, day to day fears can be eradicated in minutes or even seconds.

Better still, Richard's 'psychological technology' can be used to eliminate a wide range of problems quickly and easily and help anyone on their way to greater happiness and well-being.

This book is a wonderful distillation of many of Richard's best techniques. You can use them to help solve your problems, no matter how overwhelming they may seem, and to unleash your true potential.

Over the years I have had the opportunity to witness Richard help tens of thousands of people transform their lives. Now, in this book, the real opportunity is yours.

As you will soon discover, whatever you are working on or dealing with, this book can help you get over it, get through it or get to it!

Paul McKenna

PREFACE

I have created behavioural technologies for four decades. When I first started out in the early 1970s, the field of psychology had its therapists and practitioners fighting about who had the correct approach. The argument seemed futile to me. Over fifty schools of different theories and applications failed to produce a single consistent result. I was born into the first age of information science, and am a mathematician and scientist by trade. So, I took a different road than psychology.

I did not look for 'what went wrong' or the 'whys.' I did not look for cures. I looked at *what worked*, no matter how. If a few good therapists 'fixed' anybody, I looked at what they actually did. When people got over problems on their own, I looked at what had happened. The result is what is now called Neuro-Linguistic Programming – that is, a series of lessons that teach what others have learned that works.

I must start out by thanking the psychiatrists that helped me originally. They provided me access to clients so that I could test my work. They gave me information on those rare few clinicians – like Virginia Satir and Milton H. Erickson – who got results.

I also want to thank the courageous clients who let me teach them what I had found. For example, I looked at how more than a hundred people got over fears and studied what was common to them all. Then, I taught that process. Over these decades, I have refined and refined these procedures and, today, I believe they can help anyone to change their life.

If you're plagued with the past, stuck in a fear or just unable to get your mental motor running on time, this guide will offer a variety of ways to get your life in order. If you have spent too much time in therapy and too much money trying to do it yourself, this is for you. If you want to take control of your life, this will help you do this effectively. Just be very thorough. Do all the exercises and take careful account of the information you read. It will make a difference.

I have broken this book into three pieces.

The first part is called 'Getting Over It.'

The second part is called 'Getting Through It.'

The third part is called 'Getting To It.'

Richard Bandler

INTRODUCTION

This book is designed to be a guide for your behaviour. It is a guide to help you make changes and avoid therapy – and avoid a slow, long process of change by helping you to learn to change more quickly. One of the things that I discovered in my work is that people acquire problems very quickly. It only takes one close call in an aeroplane for somebody to get an aeroplane phobia. After one bad accident, people can get a driving phobia. It takes bees to swarm once and people become phobic of bees. If people can learn to have fear in a short period of time, there's no reason why it should take a long period of time to learn anything else, so my policy has always been to use another approach to find a quick way to do things.

What exactly was this different approach that I took? When psychologists wanted to study a particular difficulty, like phobias for example, they got together a bunch of phobics and tried to figure out why they were the way they were – effectively they looked at

what made them tick. They tried experiments, like having the phobics face their difficulties and to try and help them to desensitize their
fear over time. The psychoanalytical approach of travelling back in
time and reliving traumas, looking for deep, hidden, inner meaning
was used. This idea was based on the concept that *insight produces
change*.

This seemed like a wonderful idea! If you could understand your
problems somehow or other, they would just disappear. Sigmund
Freud started the concept and it was, at the time, a great innovation
and has been tried for some 100 years in various forms. The suggestion was that understanding the psyche could produce change. The
idea that you could help a person change verbally rather than physically was a promising insight itself. However, the idea of getting
insight into your problems just does not work.

Over the years, people have used both psychological approaches
and physical approaches. They've tried things like operant conditioning where they tried conditioning people by rewarding them for
good behaviour and negatively reinforcing bad behaviour. They
would take smokers and give them a cigarette and shock the hell
out of them. The problem is though that most people who smoke
for a while realize that it's not good for their health. They may even
know why they started smoking – to look cool in front of their friends
or to get over a nervous habit or to not eat so much – yet even though
people know why they smoke, it doesn't make them stop.

Many people also know why they have fears. I had a client who
very much understood her fears. When she was a young girl, she
was attacked, not by one person but by a group of people. She was
severely beaten. She was severely raped and developed a fear of other

people. She had a fear of going outside. In fact, she had a fear of almost everything. She'd seen a psychiatrist who treated her with therapy and drugs. I have to admit that taking valium made her more relaxed but, then again, taking narcotics makes heroin users more relaxed but it doesn't deal with the real issue.

The real issue is that they've developed a habit of being afraid, when they don't need to be. They have learned to engage in a certain behaviour that is in and of itself destructive. It destroys your quality of life. It destroys your freedom. It destroys the opportunity you have to live in a free society.

That particular girl didn't live in a terrifying place where bombs drop every day or where soldiers rape you. She wasn't being attacked and hadn't been attacked in over twenty-five years. Yet, every day, she woke up afraid. Every night she went to sleep afraid. She was afraid to meet people, afraid to date, afraid to love, afraid to work, afraid of everything.

When she came to me after all the years of therapy, it was quite by accident. She enrolled in a course with over 500 people. I have people throw notes in the box on stage about questions they have and she literally wrote down what had happened to her. She said she understood why she had a problem but still she didn't seem to be able to get away from it.

After I'd spoken to her privately, I brought her on the stage and explained to her the real truth that I didn't need to understand how she became the way she did. I needed to understand how she kept being that way. It was pretty obvious why she was the way she was – something bad happened to her and she kept reliving it and everything in the world triggered that memory.

That wasn't based on what had happened. It was based on what she did with what happened. It was based on the fact that when she woke up she was asking the question *What could go wrong?* and the same answer came up every single time. She would imagine a life-size memory where she saw the bad thing happening to her over and over and over again.

It only took me a matter of twenty minutes to get her to stop doing this because I didn't have to find out why she did what she did, I just had to get her to stop it. Better yet, I had to get her to do something more important: develop a habit of feeling happy.

If you've been afraid most of your life, you may not have good examples of what 'happy' is. In that case, you can build it in. That's what I do. You have to give people a really strong feeling of being relaxed, a really strong feeling of feeling good as a guide for their behaviour. You do this so that, in the future when they wake up, they start asking, *How much fun can I have today? How much freedom can I find? How much more can I do than I've done before?*

When people start asking good questions, they make good pictures inside their heads. If you make good pictures, you will get good feelings. Then life becomes something that you feel more enthusiasm for. This girl is a good example of how you can go from having almost no life to having a rich, full life where things get better from the top to the bottom.

In order for you to turn your own life around, it's good for you to know how all these ideas came about so that you can discover why they are so effective. When I first started out, I asked psychiatrists to name one of the toughest problems they faced and they would tell me it was phobias. So, my approach began by figuring out how to help people get over phobias and the same approach turned out to work well for other problems too.

When I studied phobias, I didn't study the people who *had* them. I studied the people who got *over* them. I found a whole bunch of people who, without any kind of therapy, had gotten over them. These people had beaten their fears. I began to interview them methodically using the tools that I had developed in writing my earliest book *The Structure of Magic: Volume One*. In this book, we discovered some of the secrets of the most successful therapists of the time and created a model of their skills. This was known as the Meta Model.

The Meta Model is a way to ask questions to find out how people process information at that time. It's not concerned with how they processed it in the past, or even how they will process it in the future, but what they do right now. *How do they manifest their fear? How is it done as an activity? How is it done over and over again as an activity?* Better yet, *How did they get over their fear? What were the steps that they took to overcome the phobia after being paralysed for years?*

A few of the people I talked to couldn't get on elevators. There were some with a phobia of bees. I had another person who had a phobia of dogs and several people who had a fear of driving. There were people with a fear of heights and a fear of open spaces. I even went to interview a few people who had agoraphobia, a fear of going outside of their home, and, suddenly, it was gone and they were able to go everywhere.

All of these people, as they told me their stories, shared certain things in common. One of which was that they reached a point where they got so fed up that they stopped thinking about what scared them and started to look at themselves being afraid and started thinking *This is really silly*. Elements like these, which they all shared in common, allowed me to develop the first 'phobia cure.' It wasn't really a 'cure' so much as a 'lesson.'

It was at that point in time that the psychiatrist that I worked with sent me droves of people with different kinds of phobias so that I could test the work that I had developed. I took the mental process of people who successfully got over phobias and I undertook *installation*. Very simply, this is the process of teaching people to think differently. Thinking isn't a passive process unless you do it passively. Thinking should always be an active process where you think in a way that gets you the results that you want.

This approach turned out to be applicable to almost all of the other problems that people had. If you can help people to think differently and actively, then they can change their lives. If you're trying to motivate yourself and you're thinking about how hard it is, it will be hard. I always say to people, *If you're looking for difficulties, you'll always find them*. If you ask the question, *What can go wrong?* then something probably will. On the other hand, if you're asking the question, *What works?* then you can find it and, in this case, I did.

Starting at about 1974, right up to the present date, I have yet to have a single individual come in with a genuine phobia and walk out with it. Many people ask me about the amount of resistance I must have faced over the past thirty-five years but I never did face very much of it for one simple reason. *What I was doing worked!*

Introduction

When you learn *how* people think, you can teach them how to change the way they think. The process that I learned from these people was something that could be recapitulated not just by me but by others. I could teach it to people in a short twenty-minute lesson. I've done it over and over again.

I made films back in the early 1980s where I took three people: one with panic attacks, one with a terrible phobia of leaving Huntington, West Virginia, and one with a fear of authority figures. Their phobias all disappeared. Each of them was treated slightly differently but each of them was taught a lesson about how to think about their fear in a new way.

When you think in a new way, you get to do new things and you get to feel new things. This whole book is about ways of thinking differently. Think about it as a lesson plan for future living. This is only one example of the things that matter when people want to make changes in their lives. You can take the process that is common to a bunch of people that successfully did something and refine it down to something that can be taught to an individual.

We also did it with simple things like spelling. When people are good spellers, it turns out that they make pictures of the words. They remember the pictures and they check them with their feelings to make sure that they're right. So, we developed an educational programme where we taught kids to look at words and we made every single letter a different colour.

After they'd looked at the words, we had them close their eyes and make a mental picture of it and then we began to ask them questions like *What colour was the third letter? What colour was the last letter?* The only way to answer those questions is to have a truly remembered image of the word and we had them check it with their feelings. We'd show them the word spelled incorrectly so they got a bad feeling with that. Then we showed it to them spelled correctly so then they got a good feeling with that. Mentally, they began to develop a process that worked.

When you see a word, you can encode the image of it. In order to remember things, you have to first encode the memory. If we teach children to properly encode the spelling of words, they'll be able to properly decode the spelling of words. The same thing is true about all memory tasks.

So the educational system was affected by my work. My work has spread all over the place. If you check out Kate Benson's website Meta4Education (www.meta4education.co.uk), you'll find all kinds of information for teachers.

There are now many books on Neuro-Linguistic Programming for the field of education. There are books on NLP applications for sports athletes. We found golfing strategies telling how great golfers are able to go into an altered state and visually adjust their body. Prize fighters and football players also use NLP to improve their performance. All people can learn to do things better.

Every task has a mental component to it. A lot of what we call talent is when people stumble upon these strategies easily. Certainly, you can't beat a good set of genes. If you're seven feet tall, it's easier to be a good basketball player. If you like basketball, it's easier to practice. If you like playing guitar, it's easier to practice but if you don't have the mental capacity of a great musician, you can begin to adjust it and to learn talent. Talent isn't just God given. It's partially

God given; the other part is accessed by human beings insofar as they're able to teach each other.

Lessons aren't just about what to learn. Lessons should be about *how* to learn. It's not enough to show a child words and ask them to remember them. You have to tell them *how* to remember them. It's not enough to go tell a phobic not to be afraid, you have to teach them what makes fear dissipate.

For almost four decades, I've gone through and I've studied everything about people with all kinds of problems. I've worked with people who were schizophrenic and have learned from people who weren't schizophrenic and who were able to do specifically what a schizophrenic was unable to do.

One of my more famous cases was brought to me by a psychiatrist a number of years ago. This was a lady who couldn't tell the difference between fantasies and memories. Every time she would come in to the psychiatrist, she would cry and moan about having killed her parents. He would bring in her parents and she would chat thoughtfully with them and when they left she would claim she had killed them.

Why she fantasized killing them isn't important. The fact is she couldn't tell which memories were real. So, I turned to the psychiatrist and asked him how he knew which one of his memories was real and which ones were fantasies. I had them both make up a memory on the spot. They both made up a fantasy of how they got to my office and put in all the necessary details and then I asked them both how they got there.

The psychiatrist answered me calmly. The patient screamed and moaned that it was one thing and then it was the other and then it was one thing and then it was the other. She couldn't tell them apart. It turned out that when I asked the psychiatrist how he knew, he told me that his fantasies had a black border around them and his memories didn't. This was a very precise way of knowing which images were created and which images were remembered. I'm sure he had no problems telling his fantasies from his reality.

I hypnotized this lady into a deep altered state and had her lift up her arm and go through the fantasies she had made up and put black borders around them. She had to do so with everything from killing her parents to any other fantasy, including the one that she had made up in the room for me. I then told her that when her brain had gone through and recoded all this information, she could let her hand come down. When she opened her eyes, I asked her if she'd killed her parents and she calmly said no.

This approach is about being able to teach people as opposed to 'therapize' them. The truth is that after all the years of giving people insight and change not occurring, the lesson to be learned was that insight was a great idea, it just didn't work. Communism was a good idea but it didn't work in practice.

When ideas don't work, you have to put them out in the backyard with the square wheels because when something isn't working, it's just not working. So, what I've tried to do over the years is find out the things that work in human beings, simple things, teachable things. Some of them are taught better in the waking state and some of them are taught better in a hypnotic trance. To me, it doesn't matter which it is, it only matters that people get to where they want to go. It matters to me that they have the freedom to live, the freedom to be happy and the freedom not to waste their time with bad habits. I believe the truth is that most ongoing problems are just a manifestation of having the same bad habit over and over again.

People with Obsessive Compulsive Disorder have the bad habit of building rituals to try and stave off their anxiety. Every single ritual may give them a little bit more comfort but in the end it continues to build more fear.

The more comfort you have to build the more fear you have to have. It's a vicious cycle and most stupidity works in this way. I'm not saying stupid in the sense that it's bad. If you discover something's stupid and you laugh at it and you stop it and build something more effective, life just gets better. I'm a firm believer that you can learn to get over your problems.

For thirty-five years, people have walked in my doorway miserable and walked out with more freedom. They have walked out happier and continue to walk out that way. People have always said, *Well this phobia cure is good but what if it comes back in six months?* Simple, you just take another twenty minutes and then you banish it again.

The truth is that it will only come back when you start doing the same things that you did before and thinking the same things as you did before. Otherwise, it will stay gone forever. In fact, something wonderful will happen. You'll have more time to get to enjoy your life.

All of the time you spent feeling bad, you could be feeling good. That doesn't mean that bad things don't happen. People die. Horrible things happen. Sometimes, people get into car wrecks or they go into debt. There are horrible things worth feeling bad about but those are things worth doing something about so that you get on with your life as quickly as you can and become the best person that you can be. You can look at yesterday and say that you are a better person today, even if it's just a tiny bit, then you're still headed in the right direction.

This book is about how you do just that. The outline of the book is very simple. First, I have outlined an inventory, which will explain the basics and help you to take stock of the tools you have at your disposal.

Next, I will discuss many of the problems that you might face in your life. You'll learn about how to get over problems such as bad fears, memories and relationships. You'll find out how to get through things like bad habits, recovery and the times when you feel like giving up. You'll discover how to get to the things that make life worthwhile such as fun, love, sex and making big decisions about your life.

Throughout the book, I'll be sharing certain stories and insights I have gained working with each problem and challenge I deal with. You'll also find plenty of techniques and tips outlined in a step-by-step guide so that, as you read, you can change instantly. Again, it's critical that you follow the steps and you do them thoroughly.

I got a postcard one time from the Grand Canyon. When I first wrote the book *The Structure of Magic*, I didn't get too many postcards. However, when I wrote the book *Frogs into Princes* that laid out ways that people could get rid of fears and anxieties, I got a postcard from the Grand Canyon.

Somebody wrote me a postcard and it simply said the following: '*I'm hanging off the side of the Grand Canyon. I had a height* *phobia for many years. I spent lots of money on therapy. But for just $8.95, my problems disappeared. Thank you.'* When I decided to write this guide so that people could get over their own problems, what I had in mind was something that would allow you all to write me a postcard.

GET THE LIFE
YOU WANT

INVENTORY

It's time to take some mental inventory. In order for you to make changes, I want to make you aware of a few mental tools that you already have at your disposal. As you proceed through this book, you'll discover more and more how you can use these tools to achieve freedom from your troubles. Once you understand how your mind works and how your thinking works, you will become aware of why you'll be able to make such powerful and permanent changes in your life. To start with, let's examine the role and the power of the unconscious mind.

THE POWER OF YOUR UNCONSCIOUS
The Freeway to Change

Think of your mind as being made up of a conscious and an unconscious portion. Your conscious mind is the part of your mind that analyses, criticizes and thinks logically all day long. It is where you put your attention. Your unconscious is the part of your mind that controls your bodily functions, from your heartbeat to your breathing. It is where all your memories are stored and where your wisdom, creativity and problem-solving capabilities reside.

When you are asleep, your conscious mind is resting and not really doing too much but your unconscious is dreaming wildly and continues to help you process what has happened during the day.

Everyone reading this book will have heard the expression *Sleep on it* as advice for tackling a problem. That's because your unconscious has the ability to help you see things from a different perspective. Your unconscious is also where most of your mental habits function. Whenever we learn to do something with our minds, it becomes automated, and so we become unconsciously skilled at it.

These skills can be skills of depressing ourselves, hesitating, stressing ourselves out or feeling terrified and hopeless. They can also be skills of feeling really good, motivating ourselves, becoming relaxed or being more confident and hopeful.

For over thirty-five years, I've spent most of my time finding out how to help people change their unconscious habits or skills so that they could start manifesting the kind of life that they want. Often, I achieve this through hypnosis. By putting a person into trance, I can help them go inside and make changes powerfully.

Trance enables you to speak directly to the unconscious portion of the person so you can help them form new habits, unconsciously. That's how Milton H. Erickson and all the great hypnotists I've studied over the years got great results. One of the best discoveries I made, however, was that it's possible to help people make these changes without hypnotizing them.

We are always in one trance or another. A trance is simply a state where we are absorbed with our thoughts. People ask me if I ever have a problem getting someone into a trance, and I never do. I sometimes have a problem getting them out of the trances that they are in, the altered states where they make stupid decisions and think stupid thoughts, but trance is an everyday phenomenon.

With the technologies I've created over the years, such as Design Human Engineering and Neuro-Hypnotic Repatterning, I've found ways that people can go ahead and make unconscious changes themselves without needing to be put into a trance. Just the process of going through the simple thought experiments in this book, will mean you find basic yet immensely powerful tools that will assist you to make changes in your own unconscious habits so that you can change your life. One of these tools we refer to as the model of submodalities.

THE QUALITIES OF YOUR THOUGHTS
Submodalities

Back in the 1970s, John Grinder and myself originated the idea that people build mental representations. It wasn't a new idea really. Gentlemen like Gregory Bateson and Marshall McLuhan had been talking about such things for years, but we formalized the idea.

We defined thinking as thinking in pictures, thinking in words, and thinking in feelings, tastes, and smells. Since then, I've taken it a step further. I've broken each of those systems down into their various components. The qualities of the images, sounds, and feelings are known as submodalities.

We have five senses that we use to take in information from the outside world. Then we represent the world to ourselves using five internal senses. When we think, one way is that we think in pictures or movies.

Whenever you get directions from someone, or you give directions to someone, it relies on your own ability to go inside and mentally represent through a movie how to get to wherever it is that you need to go. When people create anything, they must create it first in their mind by imagining what it is going to look like.

There are also certain qualities to these images. For example, think about what you did yesterday. As you think about it in your mind, you might see yourself yesterday doing something or you might see what you saw through your own eyes yesterday. You might see still images of your activities or you might remember them like a movie continuously running. Regardless, this is one way that we process our experiences from the world.

We also hear internal sounds. Whenever you remember what someone said to you or their voice or whenever you remember what a song sounds like or whenever you talk to yourself … all of these are examples of internal sounds. Again, these sounds have various qualities, such as loudness and resonance when we pay attention to them.

Internal feelings are no different. Whenever we have a feeling, we can feel it in our body in particular locations. We can feel it starting somewhere and then moving somewhere else in our body when we pay attention to it. People even describe it when they talk about fear. They will say things like *I felt butterflies in the pit of my stomach, and then my mouth went dry and I felt lightheaded.* People are constantly revealing what is going on inside their mental reality.

When we think of something, the picture of it is in a particular place. It's a particular size. It's a particular distance from us. When we look at mental images, they don't look like the same as the outside world. We do, however, seem to represent them somewhere in front of us and they are a certain size. You either see yourself in the image, which means that you are disassociated, or you don't see your-self in the image because you are looking through your own eyes. This means you are associated.

When listening to a mental voice inside your head, it's either your voice or somebody else's voice. It's either on the right or on the left. It's either going in or going out. Some of them are very loud and some of them are very quiet. Sometimes, there is just silence. It doesn't mat-ter where it is coming from and it doesn't really matter which it is but it does matter that you notice the differences that exist in the voices between different states.

People have been talking about feelings in the field of psychology for a long time. When I started, I saw all kinds of counsellors, all kinds of therapists, and all kinds of psychiatrists working with patients. What always amazed me was the number of times somebody would be asked, *Well, how do you feel about that?* and somebody would say, *I feel frustrated.* They would ask the same question again instead of finding out what that meant. They failed to stop and see that word which has been turned into an event was actually something the person was doing.

When people say they're frustrated, it's actually a verb. When peo-ple say, *I have doubts*, they've turned the verb into a noun and made it so that it becomes an event or a thing. When people say, *I have frus-tration*, they don't actually have a bucket of frustration. They're in the process of *frustrating*. That is an activity. When you turn it back into an activity, you can find out so much more about it.

So when therapists and psychiatrists say to somebody, *How do you feel about feeling frustrated?* or *How do you feel about feeling disappointed?*, they miss the most important information. We know that there's another way that we process the world. Our understanding of the endemic brain tells us that the connection between all the organs is as sophisticated as the synapses inside the brain and actually allows us to think with feelings.

What this means is that our bodies are not disconnected from our brain. They are an extended part of the brain. The important question to ask people when they say, *I feel frustrated*, is, *Where? Where does the feeling start? Where do you feel it first in your body? Where does it move to?* Feelings can't stay still. They are always moving somewhere, in some direction.

I know people sometimes feel as if they have a knot in their gut when they're frightened but in fact that knot either rotates forward or rotates backwards. Every single time somebody has told me they feel stuck and I ask where, they have told me the feeling was in their stomach or in their chest. However, it doesn't really matter where it is. It matters what you do with it.

Sometimes, I ask, *Which way is it moving?* and they say, *It's not.* It is only by having them take their hand and having them rotate it forward and backwards, to the right and to the left that we can find out which way their feelings are moving in their body. These are the only dimensions really available.

One of these directions will feel right when they think about their feeling. From this, people typically get the idea that it is moving ever so minimally. The fact that it's moving means that you can move it faster, you can move it slower, you can move it forwards and you can move it backwards. Our feelings are not outside of our control. In fact, this is the very thing most of us need to gain control of because, when you do, you can alter it.

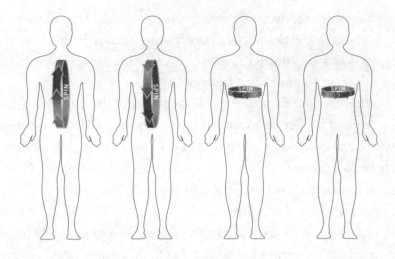

The qualities of your thoughts, these submodalities, determine how your thoughts affect you. When you make big movies of things that you are associated with, generally, the feeling will be more intense. When you make the movie smaller and move it, disassociated, into the distance, the feeling will be smaller. We can also learn how to use our control over submodalities to manifest the kinds of feelings we need when we need them. I like to call this running your own brain.

RUNNING YOUR OWN BRAIN
Changing Neurochemistry

One of my main focuses in the work that I've done has been discovering ways to help people achieve what I call Personal Freedom. Personal Freedom means having the freedom to be able to control your thoughts and to manifest the kinds of feelings you want in your life.

We are often imprisoned by the chains of our thoughts and we allow ourselves to think ourselves into problems. However, since most problems are created by our imagination and are thus imaginary, all we need are imaginary solutions. So, here are some effective ways of controlling your thinking for a change.

Think of a time when you felt really good and then start playing around with the qualities of the images, sounds and feelings. By changing these submodalities, you get to intensify the feelings.

For example, think of a time when you felt really, really good. Now, step inside that time and see through your eyes, hear through your ears, and feel the really good feeling all the way through your body. Make the images bigger, brighter, more colorful and you'll probably find yourself feeling even better. Make the sounds louder and crisper and if there are no sounds, add sounds. Start to intensify the good feeling.

Next, find out where in your body the feeling starts and where it goes. Discover the direction it spins inside your body and spin it faster and faster and, again, notice your feelings intensify. There lies the control you have over your brain to create powerful feelings inside of you.

You can then attach these feelings to other thoughts. If you keep spinning this feeling inside your body and you think about your future while it's spinning, you will start to associate the feeling with your future. By doing this, you will start to feel better about your future.

How to Feel Wonderful

1. Think of a time you felt wonderful.
2. Close your eyes and imagine that time in vivid detail. See the image clearly, hear the sounds loudly, remember the feelings like they were then.
3. Imagine yourself stepping into that experience and imagine being in that memory as if it's happening now. See what you'd see, hear what you'd hear, feel how good you'd feel. Make the colours stronger and make it brighter if that helps. Notice how you were breathing back then and breathe that way now.
4. Pay attention to the wonderful feeling in your body and get a sense of where the feeling starts, where it goes and the direction it moves

in. Imagine taking control over the feeling and spinning it faster and faster and stronger and stronger through your body as the feelings increase.

5. Think of a time in the future where you could use these good feelings. Spin these feelings throughout your body as you think about the future and the things you are doing over the next few weeks. Don't be too surprised if you find yourself feeling really good for absolutely no reason.

Similarly too, if you find yourself in a negative or unresourceful state, you can change it by changing the qualities of the feeling.

For example, think about somebody who annoys you, intimidates you or irritates you. Make an image of them and see them look at you in whatever way they look at you when they are annoying you. Hear them say whatever it is that they say and notice the bad feeling that happens in your body.

Next, take this image and make it black and white. Move it far off into the distance. Make it much smaller, one eighth its size. Place a clown's nose on their face. Hear them say whatever it is that they say but hear them say it in Mickey Mouse's, Donald Duck's, or Sylvester the Cat's voice. This changes the feeling that you have towards them and allows you to deal with them with more confidence and effectiveness.

Changing Bad Feelings

1. Think about somebody who annoys you, intimidates you, or irritates you. Make an image of them and see them look at you in whatever way they look at you when they are annoying you. Hear them say whatever it is that they say and notice the bad feeling that happens in your body.
2. Take this image and make it black and white. Move it far off into the distance. Make it much smaller, one eighth its size. Place a clown's nose on their face.
3. Hear them say whatever it is that they say but hear them say it in Mickey Mouse's, Donald Duck's, or Sylvester the Cat's voice.
4. Notice how you feel differently. Then distract yourself for a few moments and think of them again. You will still be feeling differently about them.

When you practice using your brain in this way, you will find yourself feeling really good a lot more often. This is all about developing new mental habits and skills and making it so that you get used to mentally running your brain the way you choose to run it.

The next element that I want to cover is the process of dealing with beliefs.

BUILDING NEW BELIEFS

The Structure of Certainty

One of the most important aspects of what human beings do is that they build beliefs. Beliefs are what trap most people in their problems. Unless you believe you can get over something, get through something, or get to something, there is little likelihood that you will be able to do it. Your beliefs refer to your sense of certainty on some of your thoughts.

Most people listen to their parents, teachers, and authority figures from an early age and learn lots of limitations that they supposedly have. If you were told that you were not clever enough or not good enough at a subject or at a sport, the danger is that you believed it. As soon as we believe in something, we search for ways to prove it's true. What we are looking for here is to learn to doubt your limitations and be more certain in what is possible for you.

In order to create any change, it's necessary to help the person change their beliefs and build new beliefs that will allow them to

15

maintain the change into the future. In order to change beliefs, we first need to learn a way of finding out the qualities of beliefs.

Once again, this is where submodalities come in useful. Like any thought, our beliefs have a structure in terms of their qualities. If I were to ask you, *Do you believe the sun is coming up tomorrow?*, what would your response be? Typically people immediately answer, *Yes* but there is an intervening process. In order to answer the question *Do you believe the sun is coming up tomorrow?*, they will usually represent this belief.

It's important to note that if I asked you the question verbally, you would know the answer without speaking aloud. When I say, *Is the sun coming up tomorrow?*, typically what happens is that people flash an image of the sun somewhere in their mind. They may say, *Yes* inside their heads in certain tone of voice and they will have a feeling of certainty somewhere in their body which lets them know that this is true.

This is a guide for our behaviour. It allows us to make plans. It allows us to buy a book and know that we'll read it in the future. Having beliefs as a guide to our behaviour is an important part of being a human being. It's also an important part about knowing how to change a human being, and how to change yourself in particular.

If I were to ask you verbally, *Is the sun coming up tomorrow?* where is the picture in your mind? Is it to the right or to the left? How far away is it? Is it life size or is it a small picture? Is it a still picture? Is it a moving picture? Does it have any sound? Is there any voice that says, *Yes?* Is there anything that goes on that you hear and, if so, is it on the right? Is it on the left?

Take that feeling of certainty. Look at that picture in your mind and double it in size. Typically, your feelings will get stronger. When they do, notice where the feeling is in your body and which way it's moving. You are beginning to pay attention to the submodalities of a strong belief.

Now, for a moment, stop and look away. Clear your mind and then come back to the pages and read with me.

Next, think about something that you're really unsure about. Not something you doubt utterly but something that 'maybe is' and 'maybe isn't.' Think of something you're unsure of. It could be what you are going to have for lunch? *Maybe a tuna sandwich or maybe a cheese sandwich.* Something that may or may not be the case. It could even be what somebody's going to buy you for your birthday? *Maybe it'll be this* or *maybe it'll be that.*

Look at it in your mind. Pause for a second, look away from the book and think about it. Then, come back to the book and come back to the idea of what you believe strongly. First, look at the image of the sun coming up tomorrow. Now look at the second image, what may be and what might not be. Compare the difference between the two.

First, are the images in the same place? The answer is probably no. If the images are in a different location then, are they a different distance? Are they a different size? Is the voice inside your head coming from a different place? Is one on the right, one on the left? One going in, one going out? The only part of this that makes a difference is the part where the difference lies between the two images.

You can begin to look at this difference more closely by studying the qualities of certainty and uncertainty in more depth. What follows below is a long list of submodalities: visual, auditory, kines-thetic (feeling), olfactory (smell), and gustatory (taste). What I want you to do is to go inside and access the belief of the sun coming up and the other image of what you are uncertain about and go down this list. Only check off those submodalities that are different between what you believe strongly and what you believe less strongly. Take a few moments and do this.

Discover How You Do Certainty

1. Think of something that you believe strongly. (That the sun will come up tomorrow.)
2. Notice what images, sounds, and feelings arise when you think about this belief and your certainty in it.
3. Go down through the list of submodalities below and note all the qualities of the belief.
4. Think of something that you doubt or are not sure of. (Maybe this, maybe that.)
5. Notice what images, sounds, and feelings arise when you think about this thought and your uncertainty about it.
6. Go down through the list of submodalities below and note all the qualities of the thought.
7. Note especially the differences between the strong belief and what you are uncertain of.

Differences of Submodalities:

	Certainty	Uncertainty
Number of images	_____	_____
Moving/Still	_____	_____
Size	_____	_____
Shape	_____	_____
Color/Black and white	_____	_____
Focused/Unfocused	_____	_____
Bright/Dim	_____	_____
Location in space	_____	_____
Bordered/Borderless	_____	_____
Flat/3D	_____	_____
Associated/Disassociated	_____	_____
Close/Distant	_____	_____

Auditory Submodalities:

Volume	_____	_____
Pitch	_____	_____
Timbre (mood of sound)	_____	_____
Tempo	_____	_____
Tonality	_____	_____
Duration	_____	_____
Rhythm	_____	_____
Direction of voice	_____	_____
Harmony	_____	_____

Kinesthetic Submodalities:	Certainty	Uncertainty
Location in body	_____	_____
Tactile sensations	_____	_____
Temperature	_____	_____
Pulse rate	_____	_____
Breathing rate	_____	_____
Pressure	_____	_____
Weight	_____	_____
Intensity	_____	_____
Movement/Direction	_____	_____

Olfactory/Gustatory Submodalities:		
Sweet	_____	_____
Sour	_____	_____
Bitter	_____	_____
Aroma	_____	_____
Fragrance	_____	_____
Pungency (strength of smell)	_____	_____

Now that you have your list, let's take a look at it. What you know now is the difference between what constitutes a strong belief and what constitutes something that you're unsure of. Once you know the difference between these two, you can get a semblance of control. If you're reading this book there are probably some things about yourself that you want to change, therefore the first step is to make yourself believe that you can.

Start out and think of a problem you believe you have. It doesn't matter what kind of problem it is. If you believe that you don't have enough confidence or if you believe that you're insecure, either would work. The odd thing about believing that you're insecure is that people are always secure in the knowledge that they believe that they're insecure.

For our purposes here, what we want you to do is to start out and, just like the belief that the sun is coming up tomorrow, you probably believe that you'll have this problem tomorrow. Look at your problem in the same place that your belief was and the first thing to do is to look at it and say, *I'm tired of this*. Over the years, I've discovered that the moment people really change is when they simply decide that enough is enough.

Most people are not fed up enough with their problems. They may seem to be frustrated beyond belief. I've had people with Obsessive Compulsive Disorder whose every moment, every morning, noon, and night, was consumed with rituals designed to find comfort. They had to lock and unlock the door fifteen times, wash their hands a thousand times in a day but they became so frustrated that they finally said, *Enough is Enough. I'm just not doing this any more*. This is the moment where people really change themselves. But we'll come back to this later.

The first thing that we want to do is to take a look at what it is that you want to get rid of and what you want to add. You want to get rid of your self-doubt and add more belief in yourself. You want to get rid of your fears and add more confidence. Whatever it is, when you think about your problem, you probably have believed that you were going to have it for the rest of your life.

When you look at this belief that it is going to be here for the rest of your life, I want you to do a few small things with it. Literally, push the picture off in the distance and move it over and pull it up into that place of uncertainty so, when you look at it, and you think, *Am I gonna be stuck like this for ever?* You say, *Ehhh, maybe yes, maybe no.*

In order to make it so that it sticks in any other position, it's important that you do this very, very fast. So, to make it that you can place this old, limiting belief inside your uncertainty, you have to take a hold of the image and do something with it. You have to push it all the way off so that it's twenty feet away, move it across your midline and pull it up on the other side into the submodality qualities of uncertainty so that what was a strong belief becomes uncertainty.

Then you need to do the opposite. You need to take the image of what you want to believe, such as that you will be free from this problem and happy and well in the future, and push this image out twenty feet, move it over and pull it up into the position and submodalities of your strong belief.

This allows you to change your beliefs and begin to believe in yourself and in a brighter future. When you have control over what you believe, you can start generating new, resourceful beliefs that help you to live happier and better than ever before. When you follow the steps to this exercise, you'll find yourself with a plan that you can implement to help you change your expectations of the future.

The Belief Change Technique (Belief Swish Pattern)

1. Think of a limiting belief you no longer want to have. For example, that you will have your problem for the rest of your life, or for quite a while at least.
2. Think of a resourceful belief that you do want to have. For example, that you will be free from your problem for the rest of your life and live very happily.
3. Study the submodalities of certainty and uncertainty that you have already elicited.
4. Imagine the limiting belief you want to get rid of firing off into the distance and snapping back into the submodalities of the uncertainty.
5. At the same time imagine the resourceful belief firing off into the distance and snapping back into the submodalities of the strong belief.
6. Repeat this a number of times, each time quickly.

Most problems that we face in life, as I have said already, happen in our minds. Furthermore, problems generally exist in our concept of the past and the future. The past and the future don't exist except in our minds.

When people mentally suffer, they usually do so by feeling bad about the past, feeling stuck in the present, or feeling scared or worried about the future. In language, we talk about 'getting over' things and putting things 'behind' us. We talk about getting through what's right in front of us. We talk about getting 'to' things and looking 'forward to' our future. For many, this is an indication of how they actually represent time. In order to change how we think about and process the past and the future, let's explore the concept of timelines.

TIMELINES

How You Mentally Code Time

Timelines refer to your own ability to code time. We think about time in certain ways. The images of the past will be in a different place than the images of the future. If you think about events in the past and imagine events in the future and notice where they are located in your mental space, you can draw an imaginary line from the past to the future and that will be your timeline.

For example, think about you brushing your teeth five years ago. Notice where you represent the image. Next, think about brushing your teeth one year ago. Notice the location. Think about brushing your teeth today. Again, notice where the image is. Think about brushing your teeth in one year and then again in five years. When you notice where each image is you can create an imaginary line linking all the images. This is your timeline and it shows you how you think about time spatially.

Generally, there are two main types of timelines. One is where time is spread out with the future in front of you and the past behind you and the present inside of you. This is referred to as 'in time.' The other is when the past is to the front of you located on your left, the present is straight in front of you, and the future is in front of you to your right. This is known as 'through time.'

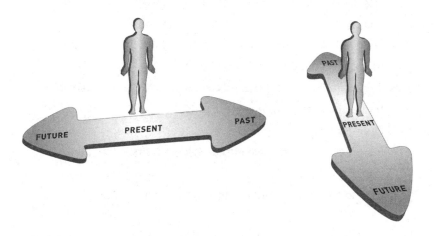

The differences between locating your timeline in these two ways are that there is usually a difference about how you approach time. For example, people who code time 'in time' generally don't remember the past very much or very often – they put the past 'behind them.' People who tend to code time 'through time' on the other hand, can usually remember incidents easily and tend to be pretty punctual.

Discover Your Timeline

1. Think of a time where you brushed your teeth *five* years ago and point to where you represent it.
2. Think of a time where you brushed your teeth *one* year ago and point to where you represent it.
3. Think of the present moment of you brushing your teeth *right now* and point to where you represent it.
4. Think of a time where you will brush your teeth *one* year in the future and point to where you represent it.
5. Think of a time where you will brush your teeth *five* years in the future and point to where you represent it.
6. Draw an imaginary line from five years ago through one year ago, the present, one year in the future to five years in the future. This is your timeline.
7. Extend the timeline further out into the future and past.

The key is in learning how you can begin to change the way you think and feel about your past, present, and future. Becoming aware, as you are now, about how you represent time makes it easier for you to change how you feel about it. Thus, your inventory is complete.

This book will focus on teaching you how to make unconscious changes by using your own brain and learning to think differently. You will be able to do this by becoming aware of how to use sub-modalities to make changes and learning how to create new feelings and attach them to new thoughts. You will also discover how to believe in yourself and a better future and you will find yourself able to change how you think about your life and all the moments of it. This inventory has introduced you to the tools and skills you will be using. Now it's time to get over your problems.

Part 1

GETTING OVER IT

In the domain of getting over things, what kinds of things do people need to get over? Let's first go down the list.

The first thing that people need to get over is bad suggestions. From the time we are born, we are told how the world works and we learn so much about ourselves, about who we are and what we're supposed to do.

We've already talked about the importance of holding useful beliefs, so it's crucial for people to learn how to get over bad suggestions so that they can start to believe in the right kinds of thing and develop new ways of thinking about the world and their future.

Another thing that people have to get over is fears. People have a fear of flying and can't get on an aeroplane. People have a fear of elevators and can't go up the easy way. Not all meetings are on the ground floor. People have fears of public speaking.

There are lots of kinds of fears that people have to get over and different approaches to different kinds of fear which we'll cover.

People have to get over bad memories. There are many different kinds of bad memories. There are people who were abused when they were young. There are people who were traumatized when they were young. I've had clients who were raped, as I mentioned earlier. Bad things happen to good people. Reliving the bad things over and over and over again is not beneficial. If doing something once makes you have fear, doing it over and over and over again is only going to reinforce that fear.

The same is true of bad relationships and grief. The more people are stuck for a long period of time feeling bad about the past, the less time they have to begin to make life more wonderful. It's important for people to know how to get over such things so that they can get on with creating new relationships and new joy in their life.

Finally, we have bad decisions that come about from bad thoughts and bad moods. It's essential that we learn how to go in the best direction in our lives – and all that begins with learning how to make good decisions. The better the decisions you make, the better your actions, the better the results in your life.

Getting over things is often about helping people to learn how to get their mind to let go of things. It means that you put your problems into the past where they belong.

GETTING OVER
Bad Suggestions

The first thing to put into your past and keep there are the bad suggestions that others have shared with you. I once had a client whose name was Myra. Myra was a cute twenty-three-year-old girl but she had a poor opinion of herself that she dressed herself up like an ugly muffin and put on the worst horn-rimmed glasses you have ever seen.

She seemed to do her hair by driving in a convertible and letting the wind pile through it. When she came in, she told me that her problem was that she was lonely. The truth was that the only reason she was lonely was that she believed, as her therapist had told her, that she had low self-esteem.

When I asked her how she knew she had low self-esteem she said, *Well I just feel nervous around people.* The truth is nobody *'just'* does anything. As I began to explore a little closer, I said, *Well, how do you know how to feel nervous? Do you feel nervous when you're in a closet picking out a shirt?* She replied, *No* and I said, *Well, how do you know when to feel nervous?* She said, *The voice tells me.* So I said, *Which voice?* She looked at me and said, *The voice inside my head.*

I said, *Is it your voice?* and she said, *Well it's inside my head.* So, I asked, *Does it sound like the voice you have on the outside?* and she said, *No.* I said, *Does it perhaps sound like your mother's voice, or your father's voice, or your sister's voice, or friend's voice at school?* And she says, *Well, I'm not sure whose voice it is. It's been there so long.* Then I said, *So long. I like that phrase. So Long Voice.*

I asked her, *What exactly does the voice say?* and she said, *The voice tells me that I'm nothing. The voice tells me I'm ugly. The voice tells me that no one will love me.* We could spend hours, in fact we could spend years, going back into her childhood finding out where it came from and why it came but I frankly didn't care. When you want a guide to changing your behaviour, you're looking for quick ways to make quick changes.

In Myra's case, I simply had her turn the volume of the voice up. She turned the volume of the voice up and moved the voice closer. The voice was actually on the left hand side and it sounded as if it was about twelve or thirteen inches away. I had it get closer and louder and she felt even worse. Then I had her move it further away and off into the distance and it diminished her feelings.

Next, I had her change the tone of the voice because I asked her a question. *Did you ever hear somebody talk that you absolutely didn't believe?* For example, Richard Nixon popped into my mind. I remember Bill Clinton telling me how he did not have sexual relations with that woman and, as he said it, I knew he was lying. As she listened to the voice, I had her slowly change the tone of the voice to somebody she absolutely distrusted and wouldn't believe.

I had her move the voice around to the back of her head so that it sounded like it was further and further behind her. Now, by doing this, not just once, but several times quickly, she got control over what was creating the bad feelings.

She hadn't tried to be pretty. She hadn't tried to speak in a cheerful voice so that she would meet nice people. Instead, she had always sought out the people that would reinforce the beliefs that she already had.

It was important not just to give her control over the voice but to change her entire belief because years of experience had taught Myra that she was a worthless, ugly, nothing of a person and the truth is that was the biggest lie of all. So, she had to think of it all as lies. When I got Myra to think differently about this old negative voice, changing the tone so that it sounded completely untrustworthy, it allowed her to be free. She managed to change how she felt about herself because she no longer took seriously her own self-criticism. Instead, she became happier with who she was.

What I like to do is to ask people what the biggest lie they've ever been told is. The one that, when they figured out it was a lie, was so much of a lie that even when they think about it now they get angry about it.

I elicit the submodalities of that just as we did in the inventory part of this book earlier. Stop now and think about something you no longer want to believe. Just like Myra, I want you to go through your list and find out first where is the voice? Where is the picture?

I want you to take the thing that you want to get rid of and I want you to compare it with the biggest lie you've ever been told. Compare it with the one you're the most angry about. Go back and forth and notice the differences in the locations of the images. Notice the difference in the size of the pictures. Whether they're movies, whether you see yourself in them. All the same distinctions that we went through in the inventory.

When you find the difference, I want you to take the thing that you no longer wish to believe and push it all the way off into the distance, move it over and pop it up on the other side so that when you look at it you know it's a lie and you're angry about it.

Then it's time to build a new belief. What would you like to believe? If you build a belief that you, like every other human being, are entitled to be happy, and are entitled to make friends, that will be much more useful. You still have to have a reference structure. You have to look at yourself and see yourself the way you'd be if you had grown up with this useful belief.

What if you were cheerful? What if you were happy? What if you realized you were pretty? Look at all those things so that you have a direction to go in. You have to change that image and change the way you sound. You might have to change the way you walk and the way you look, so much so that when you look at it, you feel intense desire. You need to have desire for the future. You need to look at the past and decide the best thing about it is that it's over.

In this guide, I'm going to say that over and over and over again. This is because the more I've gotten people through the years to believe that the best thing about the past is that it's over and that when they look at it, they may be angry about how silly they have acted and about the beliefs they had – how they learned them and who taught them – this is still not going to help them to go into the future. What helps you go into the future is to leave the past behind and to create such strong desires that you want to move towards them.

When Myra saw herself, I also gave her some suggestions. I suggested that she got some help buying clothes, she got some help putting on make-up and that she went out and looked at people who appeared to be happy and saw the way that they acted and adjusted the images in her mind until she built a whole repertoire of possibilities.

Overcoming Negative Suggestions

1. Think of something negative someone has told you or something bad you say to yourself.
2. Think of someone you distrust who has told you a lie and remember how they told you the lie.
3. Notice the submodalities of the lie and the negative suggestion.
4. Move the negative suggestion into the submodalities of the lie and snap it into place so you think about the suggestions in the same way as the lie.

Differences of Submodalities:	Bad Suggestion	Biggest Lie
Number of images	_____	_____
Moving/Still	_____	_____
Size	_____	_____
Shape	_____	_____
Colour/Black and white	_____	_____
Focused/Defocused	_____	_____
Bright/Dim	_____	_____
Location in space	_____	_____
Bordered/Borderless	_____	_____
Flat/3D	_____	_____
Associated/Disassociated	_____	_____
Close/Distant	_____	_____

Auditory Submodalities:		
Volume	_____	_____
Pitch	_____	_____
Timbre (mood of sound)	_____	_____
Tempo	_____	_____
Tonality	_____	_____
Duration	_____	_____
Rhythm	_____	_____
Direction of voice	_____	_____
Harmony	_____	_____

Kinesthetic Submodalities:	Bad Suggestion	Biggest Lie
Location in body	_____	_____
Tactile sensations	_____	_____
Temperature	_____	_____
Pulse rate	_____	_____
Breathing rate	_____	_____
Pressure	_____	_____
Weight	_____	_____
Intensity	_____	_____
Movement/Direction	_____	_____

Olfactory/Gustatory Submodalities:

Sweet	_____	_____
Sour	_____	_____
Bitter	_____	_____
Aroma	_____	_____
Fragrance	_____	_____
Pungency (strength of smell)	_____	_____

As well as giving her suggestions to help her make changes in her future, it was also useful to get Myra to think differently about herself and her past. By getting her to imagine being given a positive suggestion about how beautiful she was and making sure the suggestion was convincing, it allowed Myra to feel differently about herself.

One way to do this is to use timelines. By going back through your timeline into a time years ago when you were young and by hearing a positive suggestion that you believe and are convinced about, it helps you begin to change how you feel. When you then imagine going through your past experiences but with this new belief you will find yourself having dealt more effectively with every situation and it will literally change your personal history in ways which benefit you. When you can take on board new, positive suggestions and disbelieve the old, limiting suggestions, you will be ready to tackle the rest of your problems, especially your fears.

Building Better Suggestions (Changing Personal History)

1. Think of a more useful suggestion that you want to believe.
2. Imagine yourself floating back in your timeline to when you were very young and imagine hearing someone, very convincing that you really believed, saying to you this useful suggestion.
3. From inside this experience in the past, imagine yourself going through your timeline, through every experience from this past experience to the present with this new belief in yourself and notice how things change and how differently you feel in the light of this new belief.
4. When you get to the present day, you can repeat this with different suggestions and notice how, each time, you feel better about the past and who you are in the present.

GETTING OVER
Fears and Phobias

When it comes to getting over things, getting over fears is probably the biggest obstacle people have. Over the years, people have come to me with such a wide variety of fears and they don't all seem to work the same way.

Fears themselves fall into two main categories: phobias and anxieties. Phobic fears are when you see something and immediately you're overwhelmed with fear. Anxiety is a slower, gradual build-up of fear, where people go inside their mind and make pictures of terrible outcomes.

In terms of phobias, the steps to overcoming them are really pretty simple. People think that they're afraid of elevators. People think they're afraid of flying. People think they're afraid of driving. They're afraid of bees. They're afraid of spiders. They're afraid of snakes. They're afraid of heights.

People think they are afraid of these things, but they are not. It's not the object. It's not the height that makes you afraid, it's your brain. We know this because other people can be at the same height and they don't get afraid. The question is what is the person who feels fear doing inside their head and, even more importantly, what is the person who feels calm or confident in those situations doing inside their head? Let's have a closer look at some of these phobias.

Let's start with height phobias. Most people with a fear of heights get out of bed easily and the truth is that what starts them feeling fear is that whenever they see themselves doing something, they feel as if they are. This is a useful strategy to get out of bed. However, if you start to walk towards the edge and think that you could fall, you feel like you are falling so it creates vertigo.

For years, when I lived in San Francisco I used the Manderin Hotel to test height phobias. The best thing about the Manderin Hotel is that it has two towers and in between them very high up there is a plexiglass bridge. So not only do you have to look out from a high place, you actually have to walk across it and look down. I used this as a test when I studied how people created phobias.

I found out how people got over phobias. I interviewed hundreds of people who had gotten rid of fears on their own and they all did something in common. They reached the point where they got fed up with being afraid.

This is an important part of dealing with your fears. What you need to do is to start to look at the times you've been afraid, not as being separate, but as if they occurred back to back. What this does is something very important. It builds up your disgust. If you take five different episodes where you were embarrassed by being terrified with whatever you're afraid of, let's say it's of flying or of heights. You specifically pick five times where you felt really stupid about it.

Pick these five times where you were crippled by your fear and run the first memory and then start the second memory and then start the third memory and then the fourth memory and then the fifth memory. With each one, make the pictures bigger and closer and brighter and louder until, when you look at it, and when you see yourself in these memories, something happens. I want you to look at it to the point where you just say, *This is ridiculous.*

If you run through all five and go back to the beginning and run through all five again and go back to the beginning and run through all five again really, really fast, then what will happen is that you'll begin to feel fed up. There'll be a point where something inside you says, *Enough is enough.*

Enough is Enough Pattern (Threshold Pattern)

1. Think of five times where you felt embarrassed by having your fear.
2. Make a movie of the first time you felt this way. Then the second time, third time, fourth time, and fifth time.
3. Put all the times together one after the other in one continuous movie of you looking ridiculous, being scared with this fear.
4. Make the pictures bigger and brighter as you run the movie of all five times in a row and you see yourself looking ridiculous. Run the movie over and over again until you feel really embarrassed by yourself.
5. Do this to the point you start to say to yourself, *This is ridiculous! Enough is enough.*

The next thing you can do is to make a still image of yourself in the situation where you're afraid. Imagine you are sitting in a movie theatre with the still image on screen. Then imagine floating out of yourself in the chair so that you can look down and watch yourself, seeing yourself being afraid. Then start the movie. It's like you're in a balcony watching yourself in the theatre and you're in the film. Now as you look at yourself being afraid, I want you to stay in that third position and in your mind looking at yourself being afraid and say to yourself, *That's ridiculous*. As you look at yourself being terrified, watching yourself being terrified, something inside you will feel different.

Run all the way to the end of the episode then float back down into the theatre, float into the movie and then run it backwards so that everybody walks backwards, talks backwards and throw in a little circus music so that it's as ridiculous as it could be. Then, clear your mind for ten minutes and then go back and think of what you were afraid of. You will be amazed to discover that your fear has severely diminished if not gone entirely.

Fast Phobia Cure

1. Think of a phobia that you have. Think of a time when you experienced that phobia (or the imaginary situation that defines your phobia).
2. Imagine yourself in a movie theatre, watching yourself on the screen going through the scary experience.
3. Imagine yourself in the projector booth of the theatre, looking down and watching yourself looking at yourself in the cinema screen going through the scary experience.

4. Run the movie to the end to where you have successfully survived the experience and then imagine floating inside of yourself at the end of the movie.

5. As you stand inside yourself at the end of the scary movie, imagine running it backwards so that everything goes backwards. You are walking backwards, talking backwards, moving backwards and hear circus music in your mind as you do this until you get to the start of the movie to a point before you encountered the experience. Then think of the phobia and notice how you feel differently.

6. Repeat steps 1–5 a couple of times.

7. Notice the difference in your feelings when you do this and you think of the phobia and notice how you don't feel that phobia any more!

You can add to that a little laughter. You can, this time, look at a high place so that you immediately go to that height. I took people to the Manderin Hotel and I tickled them so that they giggled a little bit and then I led them towards the edge of the bridge and had them look down. At first as they looked down, of course, they'd feel a little trepidation but then I would have them step onto it and take another step and another step with another tickle and another laugh because everybody says that you're going to look back and laugh at your problems. My policy is, why wait? If you're going to look back and laugh, you might as well start laughing.

Laughter produces endomorphines that are an important part of changing your mind. The more you laugh at what you're afraid of, the more chemicals that go into your body. Even if it's artificial laughter, it doesn't matter. If you can stop now and look at the same picture in your mind that scared you and not be afraid, then you're ready for the next step. So, get up from your chair and go out and test it and test it and test it and, bit by bit, it will simply disappear.

Laugh Away Your Fears

1. Think of a time when you laughed your head off. One of those times where you found yourself laughing and it was impossible to stop. Remember how it felt, what you were thinking and feeling vividly.
2. Start chuckling along to yourself as you do this until you are laughing away continuously.
3. As you giggle away, start thinking of the thing you used to fear and notice as you laugh at it how it begins to change in your mind. Notice that, as you laugh, when you think about it, the submodalities of the fear change in front of your very eyes as does the way you feel about it!

As well as dealing successfully with phobias, there are effective ways of handling anxieties too. For example, let's look at the anxiety people have about public speaking. Public speaking is the single largest fear that exists on this planet. For every other fear, there are at least a hundred people who have anxiety around public speaking. I personally believe that this is a by-product of educational systems where they make children who are scared and nervous get in front of the class and have teachers attempt to humiliate them and prove that they haven't done their homework.

There are children who enjoy public speaking and join the forensics club and they learn that you can talk about anything even if you don't believe in it. They often go on to be politicians or lawyers but, for most of the people that come to me, public speaking is not something they have learned to enjoy. People who attend my charisma enhancement and trainers' courses or my public speaking courses all share in common the fact that they focus too much on themselves and not enough on what's going on in the room.

To get rid of your fear of public speaking, you have to listen to yourself talk so that you know what you're saying. I know that they teach you in school to hold up 3 x 5 cards but when you're in a meeting and discussing something with other business people or you're making a presentation to possible clients, it's not really a good idea to be holding up 3 x 5 cards.

It's a better idea to be able to watch the reactions you're getting and make sure that they're appropriate. Unfortunately, most people pay attention to the nervousness in their stomach, to the shakiness of their voice and the more they pay attention to how afraid they are, the more afraid they get. Some people are only afraid before they start and once they get going they do OK. These are people who motivate themselves through stress. They get so stressed out, then once they start talking, they start doing OK. I believe both of these approaches are totally unnecessary.

When dealing with fears, all of these things are based, for the most part, on people not paying attention to experience. It's easy to be afraid if you're thinking about the pictures in your head and you're spinning bad feelings. Whereas, if you look at the people in the audience clearly and you see them breathing in and out and you listen to the sound of your own voice, you will feel differently. Fears always have to be replaced with sensory acuity. They also can be tackled by taking control of the feeling itself.

In fact, time and time again in front of hundreds of people, I've picked somebody from the audience and brought them up onto the stage but, before they get to the stage, I ask them the important question, *Where does your fear start? When I say to you, 'I want you to come on the stage', where does your fear begin? When you think about getting in front of a group of people and speaking the most important question is where do you feel your fear?* People typically say, *In my stomach* but that's where it ends up.

The question is, *Where does it start? Does it start in your fingertips? Does it start in your forehead? Does it start in your throat or the top of your chest?* As it moves to the knot in your stomach, even for that knot to remain there it has to spin forwards or backwards, or to the right or to the left because, geometrically, those are the only possibilities.

Sometimes, it feels so tight and so stressful that people have trouble identifying these things. That's why I'm fond of having people take their finger, hold it to the side and spin it forward in a forward circle or rotate it backward in a backward circle or turn it to the right or to the left until they literally find out the direction that their fear spins in. Because once you know which direction it's spinning in, you can spin it a little faster and when you do that, you'll feel even more afraid. This isn't a bad thing. This is a good thing because it's called control.

Once you are doing this, I like people to literally visualize the circle so as they're spinning the circle forwards or backwards, whichever way the fear is moving, they see a set of red arrows moving in the

Getting Over It

direction in their mind. What happens is that you can get people to stop moving it in that way, turn the circle blue, and spin it in the reverse direction. As soon as you start to spin your fears backwards, they're no longer fears. In fact, it creates a good feeling. You spin it faster and faster and faster. Then you walk up onto the stage and turn and face people.

This isn't just a good way of getting rid of your public speaking anxiety, it's a good step to get rid of that fear of heights. It's a good step to getting rid of that fear of bees or the fear of snakes. As long as you maintain that spinning direction and spin it faster and faster and faster and faster, suddenly what happens is that the brain, at the unconscious level, begins to recode the experience. When you try to get back to having your old fear, you'll discover that it's a very difficult thing to do.

Once you have a choice, people always make the best choice. The trouble is that people don't think they have one. In order for you to discover a new choice, I recommend you try out the following exercise.

Reversing Anxiety (Neuro-Hypnotic Repatterning)

1. Think of something that makes you feel fearful or anxious.
2. Notice which direction the anxiety spins in your body and visualize it using red arrows that point which way it moves.
3. Imagine taking the feeling outside of your body, turning it around, changing the arrows from red to blue, and pulling it back in so that the feeling spins in the opposite direction in your body.

47

4. Keep spinning the feeling in the opposite direction in your body faster and faster as you notice yourself feeling differently.
5. Think of something that makes you feel really comfortable. Notice which direction this feeling moves in.
6. Spin this comfortable feeling as you imagine the experience going really well and working out perfectly.
7. As you do this, look at what you can see in front of you in the present moment, what you can hear and what are all of the things in the real world that you can pay attention to.

Most people have public speaking anxiety, as opposed to a phobia of public speaking. They slowly build up to the bad feelings by seeing things come out badly. I remember once asking somebody in an audience who'd told me that they had stage fright exactly how they did it. I'm fond of doing it in the following way. I like to tell people, *Wouldn't it be nice to have a day off from your problems? If you could hire somebody to come in and have your problems for you and you could literally live free of them, wouldn't that be great? The only problem is that you'd have to give a really good job description.*

To this particular person I said, *If I was to have your fear, I'd have to do it exactly like you. What would I have to do in my mind in order to create the kind of anxiety that you do?* Then I told them, for example, when I think about talking to an audience, I imagine an audience full of bright-eyed people just ready to learn and excited. I said, *Is that what you do?*, and of course the person shook their head and said, *No.* They told me that what they saw were little bodies with great big heads and unblinking eyes, and they literally heard themselves stuttering over words, so that they planned for how they were going to do badly. They saw an audience that was much like *Village of the Damned*, an old movie from the fifties where children hurt people. It was the precursor to things like Steven King's novels. When they learned what they were doing and they learned to practice doing what I do, they found out how they could feel differently.

Next, let's take the fear of flying, one of my favourites, since I spend so much time on planes. This is one of the fears that I encounter a lot. Being somebody that flies all over the world, I discovered that, for some reason, they always seem to sit the person with the worst fear of flying next to me. So not only have I to come up with ways to help people overcome their fear of flying, I have to do it quickly so that I don't have to listen to them whine and moan for hours in the air with white knuckles asking me if the wing is falling off.

I got a client on a plane once. There was a rock 'n' roll musician who was freaking out on an aeroplane. He even had a doctor with him who was going to administer him drugs except the musician got into a scuffle with him. When I talked to the doctor, I reassured him that in a short period of time I could make it so that flying was not so trying an event.

I sat down next to the musician and I asked him the following thing. I said, *What scares you about flying?* And he said, *When the plane bumps, I'm sure it's gonna crash! I even hear the sounds of the engines whistling and if you look out the engines are on the wings ... and they seem to be flopping up ... a wing could just fall off!* I said to him, No, *actually, it's not correct; the flexibility of the wings is what keeps them intact. If they were too rigid, they'd snap off.*

Just think about it, if you have a brittle stick and you drop it it'll crack, but if you have something that's plastic and flexible, it bends and can take a little bit of the stress.

I said, *How about clear air turbulence?* (That's where the plane bumps on something that seems to be hard.) I said, *Does that scare you?* and he said, *Oh, God! It scares the hell out of me.* So I said to him, *Well, have you ever been in a boat? The boat goes up and it hits the water, and it goes up again – does that frighten you?* And he looked at me and he said, *Of course not.* And I said to him, *Well, that's what the plane is doing, it's skidding across hard air. So, actually, it's unable to fall out of the sky. Every time it bumps, it should reassure you, that the plane is bumping up because if it didn't bump it could drop straight down.*

Then, I had him close his eyes and go inside and take the feeling of fear in his body and spin it once again a little bit faster and then turn it around and spin it backwards until it softened. I told him to relax and to be in comfort and to open his eyes and look at the flexibility of the wing and to hear the sounds of the engines. I told him to see himself being able to fly smoothly, to look off at the clouds and to realize that flying's one of the safest things you can do. You're more likely to be hit by a car crossing the street. So it's a good thing he wasn't outside the plane. Instead, inside he was safe. Even if we hit a little clear air turbulence, it just means that the plane is bouncing up.

Over the years, I've got rid of fears, phobias, and anxieties of many kinds. The exercises that we're laying out for you here show you different ways to deal with fear and anxiety. Now, if you go through each of these and you do it this way and do it that way and do it a third way, you'll be able to find the best and quickest way to get rid of your own fears.

Each and every one of the exercises in this book is designed to get you to think differently so that you can decide some things are well worth being afraid of. If you don't know about snakes and don't know which ones are poisonous, you're better off being afraid if your fear gets you to stay away from them. Some people should be afraid of the refrigerator door. Some people should be afraid of the salesman that calls on the phone.

It's not that fear is a bad thing. Fear moves you away from things; you shouldn't touch hot fire. Even when children are young, they are born with only two natural fears: a fear of loud noises and a fear of falling. That's why when children start to do something that's dangerous, we yell at them. And that fear then translates so that, instead of having to stick your hand in fire, you feel fear as you reach towards it. This teaches us and we generalize one fear to another till we learn 'don't cross the street until you know it's safe to do so.'

We learn the fear that snaps us away from touching fire, from stabbing ourselves with scissors, from poking ourselves in the eye, and we learn things that move us in the right direction. When our fears become too grandiose and too generalized, we become afraid of the wrong things. One of the things you should never, ever, ever be afraid of is your own thoughts. When you think things that scare you, you just need to think about them differently. You need to put in different sounds. You need to shrink them down. You need to learn that you are in control of how you think. This includes how you think about your past.

GETTING OVER
Bad Memories

The next thing we need to discuss in helping people to get over things is bad memories. This includes Holocaust victims, rape victims, and victims of crime, grief and death. All of the bad memories that we hold on to are made possible by the way in which we hold on to them.

It is especially important to deal with memories that haunt you on a repeated basis. Most bad memories are life size, and when you have life size bad memories, shrinking them down, putting yourself in them so you can see exactly what you were wearing (and turning the picture sideways and then being able to play that memory forwards and then backwards) will help you change the way you feel about them.

Being able to play these memories forwards with circus music and backwards with silly music makes it so that the feelings become separated from the images and the memories no longer haunt you. The purpose of memories is to learn from them or to enjoy them or to use them as guides for your behaviour and it doesn't help to relive trauma. Over the years, I've helped many, many people whose lives had been crippled by traumatic experiences to get away from the memories.

For example, recently I worked with a woman who had been terribly abused when she was young. She'd been gang raped. A terrible, terrible thing. What was even worse was that she relived it every day not once but over and over again. It made it so that she constantly lived in fear. Her body was racked with stress. Her mind was unable to think about anything, especially the future and especially hope.

It was impossible for her to carry on relationships because everything that happened triggered off the one bad memory. Even though it had happened over twenty years earlier, she was still paralysed by the pictures in her mind, the sounds, the smells and, worst of all, the feelings of helplessness and being out of control. Rape is not about sex. Rape is about violence and anytime violence is done to anyone, it's a horrible thing.

I know that I'm fond of saying this over and over again but the best thing about the past is that it's over and when it's not over something is amiss in your mind because it's not the rapist that's making you remember – it's you. Inside your own mind, holding on to terrible memories. None of us are exempt from this. When my wife died some four years ago, she died in my arms. The memory stuck with me over and over again and I was forced to take my own advice.

Step one for getting over bad memories is to look at them for the last time in the same way. One of the things that you'll notice about bad memories is that they're life size. They're not a little picture in your mind. They're not blurry. They're not out of focus. They're just like being there in that moment again.

Whenever people have trouble letting go of good things or bad things, it's because they are associated to the memory. It doesn't matter what it is, it's just like being there. If you're holding on to bad memories, it's now time to look at them and shrink them down.

Another thing to do is to freeze frame the memory. I know that it sounds crazy at first but the best thing to do then is to jump to the end, freeze frame it and literally grab a whiteness knob in your mind and turn it real quickly so that it goes blank out white, phhhhhp. Really quickly, so that the whiteness literally replaces the memory, and makes it so that you can't see it.

It's like taking the brightness knob on an old television and turning it suddenly all the way up or using that white fade out on your camera. You do this two or three times and then very slowly bring the picture back into focus, only now make it so that it's maybe eight inches by eight inches.

Look at the last image and then run it backwards to the beginning so that people walk backwards, so that the sounds are like playing a tape recorder backwards. In fact, if you can, spin your feelings in the reverse direction.

As I've already talked about, feelings always tumble forwards or tumble backwards. Remember, sometimes they feel like a knot inside your stomach but even a knot couldn't remain still or else it would habituate. So if you move your hand in a forwards circle, a backwards circle, to the right or to the left, you'll find out the direction of the motion that allows you to maintain your bad feelings – and literally freeze those and turn them in reverse, make the pictures move in reverse, make the sounds sound like they're in reverse.

Make it happen really quickly like you're rewinding a movie right back to the beginning and then project yourself outside the image so that you can see yourself unhappy. See yourself being tortured but it's a little picture and then move it off into the distance.

Changing Your Bad Memories

1. Think of a memory that you want to stop thinking about.
2. Notice the submodalities. Freeze frame it and shrink it in size.
3. Skip to the end of the memory and freeze frame it and imagine a whiteness knob and grab it, whiting it out really quickly.
4. Repeat this three times.
5. See yourself in the end of the movie and run the movie backwards, seeing the sights backwards and the sounds backwards and spin the feelings in your body in the opposite direction.
6. When you try and think of the bad memories, the more you do this the harder it is for you to remember them.

It may take a few tries at this because habits develop over years, but it will be effective. For years and years, this particular woman had run the same life size movie in her head over and over again. It became a habit. What you need to do is break it up. If you can make it small enough or, if you can, white it out often enough that will make a difference. If you can run it backwards enough that will change the feeling. You can also disassociate it. You do this by putting yourself in the picture and pushing it off into the distance. Then you can go inside your mind and replace it with something else because it's not enough to get over the past, you have to start to look at what you want in the future.

This particular woman had lacked self-confidence as a result of what had happened to her. That's not a good thing. I had her look at herself being the way she would want to be. It's not that she was there at that moment so pretending wasn't going to do any good. Instead, she needed to literally make an image in her mind that she's so drawn to and she looks at it and goes, *That's what I want*. That will help her feel desire.

When she looks at that picture, that's the picture that we want to make life size. We want to make it bigger. We want to make it brighter. We want to make it so that it surrounds her all around, so that when she looks at it every fibre of her says, *Yes, I desire this*.

Next, go back to the first bad image. Not the life size one but the little one and push it off into the distance and suddenly pull up the new picture in its place and then make it life size. So that you look at how you want to be and you end up replacing your fears with your desires.

It's a mechanical function because you need to talk to your neurology. You need to tell it what you want it to see, what you want it to feel and whenever it shows you a picture from the past that you don't like, you need to make it an instinct to white it out and to put up a picture from your future of how you want to be.

This will instruct your neurology which direction to go in. There is a tendency for some people to look at the past over and over again. Even in therapy, people going through it over and over again instruct the neurology that this is what you want. Until you start to look ahead with desire, it's very hard to get away from the past. The more you look at the bad things, the more you relive the bad things, the more familiar it gets.

The strongest instinct in human beings is not survival. Virginia Satir said to me something that has resonated with me for forty years. She said, *What do you think is the strongest instinct?* Like a robot I responded, *Survival.* For me, it had always been the strongest instinct. She said, *No, Richard. The strongest instinct in human beings is the need to look at the familiar.* People are terrified of the unknown. In fact, sometimes people will rather kill themselves than look at new things.

I was reminded of a husband once. I met his wife. She'd been in therapy for a long time. When she told them that they were through and they were getting a divorce, he sneaked into the house and hung himself in the closet and left a note that said: *I can't face a future without you.* That sums it up in a nutshell. He couldn't look into the unknown.

He couldn't look into his future and see that there would be other women and other times and other fun. He just looked at what wasn't there and when he looked at what wasn't there, his fear and his inability to make it familiar caused him such pain that it was easier to kill himself than it was to face the unknown. We have a need to make things familiar. It was familiar to him every day, all day long to look at this pain so you need to break it up mentally.

The techniques that I'm describing to you aren't techniques that you just do once but things that you run over and over and over in your mind till they become familiar to move away from pain and move towards hope. The more you move away from pain and white out your pain and see yourself in your pain – and the more you look at yourself doing the things that you want to do – the more that you'll begin to change your direction.

The same woman who was raped doesn't relive her bad memories any more. By getting her to white them out, to shrink down the life size ones, she gets freedom. When you make the images small, they're easier to handle. When you look at the little tiny TV, it's harder to get involved than a big giant movie screen. The same thing is not just true on the outside, it's true on the inside.

Also, I made it so that when she looked at her bad memories, they had a tendency to run backwards and I even had her put a little circus music in so that it would drown out the horrible sounds backwards or forwards. When she listened to the circus music and saw the people walking backwards and talking backwards she had to laugh because it looked silly.

Laughter releases endomorphines. If you can't laugh at your past, you'll never get free of it. So it's time to start laughing, even if it's artificial laughter at first. Put a little circus music in, add a little chaos and move things backwards. If they start to move forwards blank them out with white and then pull up an image of something that you really desire. Put your hopes and dreams in front of your nightmares and your terrors and your problems. A psychiatrist may call this repression. I call it planning. You should too.

Feeling Better in the Right Times

1. Think of your timeline and imagine floating above your timeline so you can see your past running to your future.
2. Imagine a time where you felt absolutely wonderful, where you laughed and you felt like everything was going to be alright, that life was wonderful.
3. Remember it vividly and spin this great feeling inside you. Once you have done this imagine yourself back above your timeline with this feeling in your possession.
4. Give this feeling a colour and imagine having a powerful hose with this feeling in it ready to burst out. Look down at your past.
5. In your past see your past stretching out to the time you were born and see all the memories you have ever had. Notice the bad memories are all coloured black.
6. From above your timeline, imagine firing this feeling through your hose at your past and cleaning all of your experiences including the black memories and watch as they change colour and no longer look the same.
7. Imagine floating back into the present and look towards the future and again fire this feeling all the way through your future so you start to get more and more excited about it and feel really great about what lies in store for you.

GETTING OVER

Grief

The next subject I want to discuss is grief. Grief is a natural process when somebody dies and we all grieve and that's appropriate, to a certain extent. In the early stages, it's important that you get *through* grief. However, over the years, again and again, I've had clients that were still grieving three, four, five, even twenty-five, thirty-five, and forty years later.

There comes a point at which grief isn't healthy anymore. Certainly, when you're married to someone for a long time and they pass away, your thoughts of them are going to be there forever. When people lose a child, they are, of course, going to hurt and they're going to hurt for a long time. Their thoughts of their child will always be there but they don't have to hurt forever.

In fact, one of the cases I had was a woman who came to me who had had four children. Her sixteen-year-old boy had died of cancer, which was a long, drawn-out and painful process. She went to pieces. Her husband brought her to me and said that the family was falling apart. All she did was cry and grieve. When I asked how long he had been dead, he replied, *Three years*. I made a decision at that point in time that I had to do something to shock her a little bit, to wake her up out of her grief and get her to pay attention to the other children she had.

The question I asked her is one that's worth considering for almost anybody that loses somebody and grieves over them. The question is simple. I turned to her and I asked her if she would rather I put her in a hypnotic trance and give her amnesia, so it would be like she had never known her son. Would she give up all the memories of his sixteen years of life in exchange for not feeling the pain that she had now? She looked at me quite angrily and said, *No* and I said, *Good. The reason you don't want to give up those memories is because if you gave yourself amnesia from ever having known somebody you loved, you'd miss out on all the good times. In fact, that's what's happening now.*

When you took inventory, one of the things that happened was that some of the images you made in your mind were images where you saw what happened at the time as if you were there. These images are associated. Some of those images, you saw yourself in those memories and those are entirely different because they are disassociated.

The trouble with long, drawn-out deaths – in fact, all deaths – is when people remember the person who has died and they make life size images and they see those images as if they're happening now. It's very difficult to get through the pain of death. When people look at good memories, they'll see themselves in the good memories, but they'll remember the funeral. They'll remember the death as if it's happening now. In other words, they'll be associated with it, and this is simply backwards. The process of flipping pictures is how people come out of grief when they stop remembering the tragedy of death and start remembering the good times vividly and associating with good memories.

What I did is I put her into a light, closed-eye process. I had her go through and take ten really good memories and see what she saw at the time and hear what she heard, and then look at the unpleasant memories and see herself worrying next to the hospital bed of her son. By going back and forth between these things, it tells us unconsciously how to sort our memories so that we disassociate from the unpleasantness of someone's death and associate with the good memories. And then there's only one more step, which is to put it in your past.

As we described in the inventory, we all have ways of sorting out where the future is and where the past is. And if you think of something that happened six months ago and something that happened a year ago and something that happened five years ago, and literally draw a line in your mind between those memories, you'll discover that there's a distance. We all measure time with distance in one form or another.

The trick is to take the bad memories and to push them off into the distance, so that they get into the past, where they belong. If we hold on to memories, as if they're happening to us now, then it's very hard for us to get over grief, and into the natural process of healing. We need to do what's important which is, once again, to come back to your senses and look at the people that are still around you. Because, everybody's got some friends, everybody's got some relatives, and even older people who have lost the people that they have loved, a husband of fifty years, need to realize there's still life out there. There are still other people.

The best thing about the future is that it's in front of you. The best thing about the past is that it lies behind.

Getting Over Grieving

1. Think of all the memories you have of the person that has passed away.
2. Remember all the good memories about being with them by being associated in the memories. Feel them as if they are happening now.
3. Remember all the bad times by looking at yourself in the image. See yourself going through the experiences in small images which are like watching yourself on a small, black and white television screen.
4. Take your timeline and imagine a line stretching way behind you which represents certain times from your past that you have forgotten and never think about. Imagine taking all of the bad times with this person and placing them all on this line way off behind you.
5. Imagine a wonderful future in front of you where you honour their memory by living as fully and as happily as possible.

GETTING OVER
Bad Relationships

The next thing that some people need to get over is bad relationships. I recommend that, when it comes to bad relationships, you decide, first off, to build a new belief that you deserve to have a good life. This is so important but most people don't do this enough.

For a while, I worked in a shelter for battered women. What amazed me most about it was the following: These women had been beaten up, bruised, and given black eyes. They were sitting huddled, shivering in the corner with their children, homeless for a time and afraid to go back to a drunken husband who had beaten them, not once but repeatedly. What amazed me was that still they would look at you and when I'd say, *You need to divorce him. You need to stay away from him for ever and keep your children safe,* they would say, *But I love him.* Either that, or else they would be sure they were going to leave him and, six months later, they would be back in the shelter again having been beaten up again.

When we're in relationships that aren't working, it doesn't require a slap on the side of the head just to get people to get over them. Sometimes people need to learn to fall out of love. One of the more famous cases I had in the beginning of my career was a guy we called Old Piney. We called him that because he came in and sat down and said he'd been pining away for the same woman for ten years and that his whole life revolved around her.

As it turns out, he would be what we would now call a stalker, because the truth is he'd never even spoken to her. He didn't know her enough to actually fall in love with her, but he'd watched her from afar in college. In fact, it was junior college. She went on to become a successful musician and he pined away about a relationship that never was and actually could never be. His idea of the perfect woman she was, was actually kind of silly because, as it turned out, one of my friends was dating her and she wasn't at all like the picture that Old Piney had in his mind. His ability to get over her and fall out of love was just as important as a woman who's being beaten and has to get out of a bad relationship, or worse, any kind of abusive relationship.

They say that some relationships are enabling relationships, where people become co-dependent with someone. If a relationship isn't built on two people becoming healthier together, happier together, building good memories, and building a good life together, then one partner just drains the life out of the other, one way or another. It either happens that way or worse, one person ends a relationship and the other just stays in love and just pines away.

All of these are examples where people need to learn to fall out of love. Falling in love is important but people seem to be pretty good at that. However, some of us are very good at falling out of love when it's inappropriate. I've had relationships that didn't even make it through lunch. Yet, when I found the right woman I stayed married for many, many years. When she died, it took me four years to find somebody else. But if I couldn't put her in my past, I wouldn't be able to put somebody new in my future.

It's always sad when somebody dies and you expected to spend your whole life with them. However, there comes a point in time where you have to hold on to the good memories and let go of the bad ones, and look forward and build new, good memories. Sometimes the person doesn't die, they just don't like you anymore and they leave you. If you stay in love, you deprive yourself of the opportunity of re-aiming your life so that you find just the right person.

Keep in mind that there are six and a half billion people on planet earth and so many of them are lonely that it's absolutely astronomical. But yet, people look to me and they say, *I'll never be able to find someone to love again.* In fact, I had a woman who was some thirty-odd years married to the same guy, and he went through a midlife crisis and ran off with his blonde secretary.

When she told me this, she had tears in her eyes. She looked at me and said, *I expected to spend my whole life with him.* She was angry. She was hurt. She was distraught, and when she looked at me she said, *Why are you smiling?* I looked back at her and said, *It's really very simple, dear. Most women can't pick a man that lasts for a whole evening. You were able to make good enough judgments to pick one that lasted for thirty years. Now that means, at your present age, you probably only have to find one more. Maybe two if you live to be a hundred. So really, you're in the position to do a good job but all you need to do is to put him in the past. And I'll tell you the secret beyond secret.*

The secret is that when it's time to fall out of love, it's called a threshold pattern. Threshold patterns are just like becoming fed up with being phobic. It's the same pattern. I talked to a lot of women that fell out of love without my help so I could figure out what they did. When women fall out of love, they reach a threshold. I had a couple of my friends who said to me, *I don't get it. I was married for seven years and no matter what I did she put up with it. And now suddenly she's just left me and she wants nothing to do with me.*

This is an example of where somebody fell out of love on their own. I went and enquired about it because I wanted to know how to help those people who really needed to fall out of love. It turns out that it's really quite simple. If a guy does something unpleasant, or a woman does something unpleasant, you can forgive them. But if they do too many unpleasant things, too close together in time, it builds up the negative feeling and you begin to hear the phrase, *It was the straw that broke the camel's back.*

What we want to do is get that straw in just the right place and snap that camel's back on purpose at just the right time. The way to do this is really quite simple. If you have a guy who's been unpleasant to you or a woman who's been unpleasant to you but they just didn't do it often enough, close enough together in time, you do the following: You go back and you take memories, at least five or maybe ten. You take these memories, make them life size so that you see what you saw at the time and you run them end to end, like they're happening now.

You go through one memory from beginning to end and, as soon as it ends, you start the next one. Sometimes, it's a good idea to write down what the five memories are. Make sure you remember where they start. Run through them very quickly so that you get them all connected together. Then you go through them in your mind, add sound and take the feelings – all the unpleasantness – and literally spin it faster and harder throughout your body.

Make the pictures bigger than life size and run them from one end to the other so that continuously you run through five bad memories, maybe ten bad memories back to back. What will happen is, you'll hit the point where your pictures will flip and your feelings will change. This is because the way in which people stay in love is much like grief in the sense that what you associate with and what you disassociate from determines how you'll move in the future.

When you get to the end of these five or ten memories, you go back to all the good memories you had with this person and see yourself being happy and shrink the picture down so that it's small. Run the movie so that it runs backwards. Start at the end of the good memories and run towards the beginning so that you're deeply in love and then you get to the point that you don't know the person.

Literally, by artificially manipulating the pictures and the sounds inside your head, it changes the way you feel. When you look at the unpleasant memories, you bring them big and close and see what you saw when this person did the things you didn't like. It always helps to add a bad feeling because sometimes people forget just how bad relationships can be. They forget how scared they were or how unhappy they were so when they think about going back with some-body, they think it's going to be good.

Some time ago, a friend of mine who's actually quite a famous person told me that they kept falling in love with the same person over and over again and the woman would run off with somebody else, hurt his feelings and then, six months later, he would end up with her again. He was really tired of her abuse. I ran him through the same process that I'm telling each and every one of you about now until he got to the point where the pictures had flipped and he got to the threshold.

Then I asked him to think of what he thought was the most dis-gusting thing he had ever seen on planet earth and he looked at me and said, *Chopped liver – just the smell of it, the sight of it makes me want to puke.* I had him look at a big plate of chopped liver and smell it until he got that bad feeling. In the centre of that picture, I had him open up a picture of her smiling face to the point that every time he thought about her, it turned into chopped liver.

Our ability to associate good feelings with things or bad feel-ings with things should be a conscious choice. When you redirect your own thoughts, when you decide what memories to associate with and what memories to disassociate with, when you manipu-late your thoughts deliberately, it is called thinking. We are think-ing beings when we think deliberately. When we let our thoughts just happen to us, we lose our personal freedom.

Falling Out of Love Pattern

1. Think of the person that you want to fall out of love with.
2. Remember all the good memories about being with them by seeing yourself in the memories. See the movies run backwards and make them all in black and white and small.
3. Remember all the times they treated you badly and all the negative feelings around them by imagining yourself looking at them inside the image, fully associated.
4. Take every bad thing they did and imagine all of them, one after another as if played back to back on a movie screen. Run this movie over and over till you get sick of them.
5. Take something that is disgusting to you and then move the image of the person into the submodalities of the disgusting image.
6. Imagine a wonderful future free of them and imagine yourself being happy and free and step into that image.

GETTING OVER
Bad Decisions

Every day, we are bombarded with thousands and thousands of choices. We are left to make many decisions, small ones and big ones. Some of these decisions won't really affect things that much and some will completely transform your life.

Getting over bad decisions is essential to move on in life. In order for you to do better, you need to make sure you are making better decisions. One factor that is important in making good decisions is the state of your thoughts.

Bad thoughts come in lots of forms. The kinds of bad thoughts that I'm dealing with here are the kinds that get you to do things that you *really* don't want to do. Getting over bad thoughts is an important part of the process. When you think bad thoughts, you feel bad. When you feel bad, you will make bad decisions. Hence, being in a bad mood is something that is not conducive to making good decisions.

71

So the first trick to making better decisions is to learn to make them when you feel good. What that means is that you start to manifest good states when you need them and develop the skill of getting over bad moods.

Getting past bad thoughts and getting over a bad mood can be accomplished by changing your state and changing your thoughts. When you go inside yourself and notice what you are doing in a bad mood and change it, you will find yourself feeling a lot better. For example, often we say nasty things to ourselves and criticize ourselves continuously. To change this, we can learn to interrupt these negative thought patterns by repeating a mantra. My favourite mantra is 'Shut the Fuck Up' because it works so well. By using strong language it lets me impact people more powerfully and it's extremely effective. Also, it literally tells people what to do. Sometimes, it's necessary to take full control over what you are saying to yourself. Then, it's useful to replace it with something better and something that works more successfully.

Eliminating Bad Thoughts

1. Notice what kinds of bad thoughts are running through your mind and what you say to yourself that makes you feel bad.
2. While you are speaking badly to yourself, repeat the mantra, 'Shut the fuck up, shut the fuck up', over and over again.
3. Each time you are speaking negatively to yourself, repeat this mantra.
4. Start saying nicer, more encouraging things and compliments to yourself in a kind and certain tone of voice.

As well as talking to ourselves, we also make images inside our heads. If you change the qualities of the images you make and you replace them with different thoughts that make you feel good, you will start to feel differently. If you physically move around and get yourself into a very different physiological state, then you will feel differently. Once you feel differently, you will be in a better position to think things through more cleverly. When you feel good, you tend to make good decisions.

Changing Your Mood

1. When you are in a bad mood, three things will be happening. You will be making images that make you feel bad, talking to yourself in a pessimistic way, and feeling bad. Notice the images, sounds, and feelings inside your head.

2. Thinking about what you want to do, figure out what is the most useful state for you to be in.

3. Move the negative images away and replace them with positive images that make you feel the way you want to feel.

4. Use the mantra to shut off your negative internal voice saying whatever it says to make you feel bad. Replace it with good suggestions, statements, encouragement, and compliments to yourself.

5. Notice what direction the feeling is spinning. Spin the feeling in the opposite direction.

6. Change around your physiology. Move about and breathe differently and imagine a time when you felt fantastic. See what you saw, hear what you heard, and spin the feeling strongly through your body.

The next step towards making good decisions is to learn the difference between good and bad decisions. For example, when people go to all the trouble of going to drug rehabilitation, they've been straight for three or four weeks. Then they leave rehab and they tell themselves, *Well, I'll just have one drink*. They know better, yet they do it anyway. They lie to themselves and say, *Well, I can handle it. I'll take one more shot of heroin, it won't hurt me*.

Most of these fall into the category of bad decisions rather than bad thoughts. Making bad decisions is really a serious problem for most of the people who end up coming to me. I think that all of us make good decisions and all of us make bad decisions. The real trick is in telling which one is which.

I get people to sit down and I have them think of one of the worst decisions they've ever made. Then I have them think of a good decision that they made and start to go through and take inventory, to notice the difference between where the images of good things are, and where the images of bad things are.

They must go down the list. Which one's closer? Which one's in colour? Which one's in black and white? They do so in order to notice the differences. Which way does the feeling move for a good decision? Which way does it move for a bad decision? You sort out the differences between the images and you sort out the differences between the locations of the voices and what kinds of things they're saying. Does the voice sound like it's going in or coming out? Does it sound close to your face or does it sound far away?

All of these are the ways in which we think about things. The decisions we make that are bad ones are uniquely different from the ones we make that are really good ones. Of course, there's that grey area in between, but mostly that's because we haven't thought about it enough that it's landed in the 'bad decision' or 'good decision' zone.

Lots and lots of people make bad decisions and act on them. These decisions work in a particular way. I have worked with people who were addicted to heroin. This is a bad decision because it means being addicted to a drug that will slowly kill you, destroy your life, make you rob stores, steal from your family, and literally ruin your health. Add to this that just a little overdose will kill you in a cold second. Yet most heroin addicts don't stop and think, *Gee, now that I've gone through rehab and gotten over the physical addiction, maybe I should never take this again.*

The same thing is true about cocaine addicts and many other kinds of addictions. Some people are just addicted to cutting their own wrists, to cutting and making stabbing marks on their body. They think that it won't really hurt them in the long run. Some people think that if they keep eating and eating and eating, then that's a good idea. They think, *If I just have this chicken, I'll feel better.* The truth is that they won't really feel better for the rest of their life.

Making decisions about what to do *now* should be based on a movie inside your mind that is appropriate to the decision. It should neither be too long nor should it be too short. If it's too long, people tend to find it hard to make any kind of decision and they over-analyse everything. If it's too short, that sometimes leads to people making poor decisions because they don't think about things enough and evaluate the consequences effectively.

I have discovered that most drug addicts didn't see themselves in the images, they just made images of the drug, life size, and remembered the little rush they got from taking it. They didn't play the rest of the movie. They didn't imagine about how much trouble it was to go through it, how much trouble it was to come down from it, the pain of withdrawal, having to get the money to buy more, and having to make the connections. Actually, being a drug addict is a tremendous amount of work. It requires tremendous effort, tremendous dedication. People wouldn't have the energy to be addicts except that withdrawal symptoms can be so motivating to get people to go out and rob liquor stores and do all those things.

Even if it's a little addiction habit or if it's just too many beers, deep down, you know that it's important to get more control of it. Some people don't consider the impact. They think to themselves, *One more isn't going to hurt,* when they know better. It is because you haven't really stopped and looked at it as a good decision. Because if you look at the differences between your good decisions and your bad decisions, if you take a look at them right now, and notice the difference in location, the difference in size, the bad decisions have repeatedly produced for you decisions which have gotten you to act inappropriately.

Being able to adjust this is important. The first decision you make – *Should I have another shot of heroin?* – you look at it and you put it in the 'Good Decision' category, and you'll find out it doesn't fit there. Next, what would be a good decision? If you look at your decision and you begin to lengthen the movie, first you see yourself in it, then you make that movie so that it's a *long* one, six months long. It will make a difference.

You will see how you have to take heroin not just once and get a little high, but you have to take it over and over and over again and have to steal money, have to make phone calls, you run out of money, you go through withdrawal in some alley shaking like a leaf, and some guy comes out and pisses in your face, until you think, *Do I really want to take that hit of heroin? Do I really want to take this?*

Suddenly the answer will be, *No!* We have an ability to tilt the scales mentally on the good decisions and bad decisions, because if you look at it as just, *Oh, well I'm feeling a little anxiety, if I eat a little chocolate cake I'll feel better,* then that might not help. But if you make it not one piece but a *thousand* pieces of cake and you feel yourself ballooning up and people laughing at you everywhere you go because you're so overweight, that will help you feel differently.

If you imagine being depressed every night and being lonely and miserable, having regrets about everything you've eaten in your whole life, and dieting and losing weight, and gaining it and losing weight, and gaining it – and then you decide – *Should I eat this one piece of cake?* The answer will be different if you say, *Oh, well, it'll make me feel better for five minutes* versus, *Will it make me feel better for the rest of my life?*

Decisions, when they're taken out of context, are something that it is important to look at. It's easy to make a bad decision especially if you ask, *Should I have three more beers? Should I drink a six-pack of beer?* Well, you don't make decisions that way. It really should be, *Am I going to be feeling good all of tonight? Am I going to get in fights? Am I going to crash my car?*

When people are drunk and they make decisions, it is too late. Instead, they should decide before they leave the house whether or not they're going to be sober enough to drive home. If you decide when you're leaving, *Well, I'll just have one beer,* then you get to the bar and you say, *Well, I'll just have one more beer*, you haven't made decisions and stuck to them. But yet everybody, without exception, has made decisions that they've stuck to for the rest of their life.

That's what we are going to look at. I'm going to give you an exercise that is about making decisions. Good decisions versus bad decisions. Decisions that you've stuck to versus decisions that you haven't stuck to. Once you know the secret of the difference between these things, it will become easier and easier to make good decisions that you follow through with. What this will lead to is that bad thoughts will no longer be bad thoughts, but will be thoughts that will trigger for you that it's time to stop thinking bad thoughts and start making good decisions.

Make Good Decisions

1. Think of a time you made a really good decision.
2. Elicit the submodalities in the section below.
3. Think of a time you made a bad decision.
4. Elicit the submodalities in the section below.
5. Think of a decision you are to make. Try thinking of your various choices and notice if they belong in the good decision submodalities or the bad decision submodalities.
6. Make sure that you think through the different potential outcomes of the decision and that it is your best option. Then decide it and stick to your decision unless it becomes more useful to decide something else.

Differences of Submodalities:	Good decision	Bad Decision
Number of images	_____	_____
Moving/Still	_____	_____
Size	_____	_____
Shape	_____	_____
Colour/Black and white	_____	_____
Focused/Defocused	_____	_____
Bright/Dim	_____	_____
Location in space	_____	_____
Bordered/Borderless	_____	_____
Flat/3D	_____	_____
Associated/Disassociated	_____	_____
Close/Distant	_____	_____

Auditory Submodalities:

	Good decision	Bad Decision
Volume	_____	_____
Pitch	_____	_____
Timbre	_____	_____
Tempo	_____	_____
Tonality	_____	_____
Duration	_____	_____
Rhythm	_____	_____
Direction of voice	_____	_____
Harmony	_____	_____

Kinesthetic Submodalities:	Good decision	Bad decision
Location in body	_____	_____
Tactile sensations	_____	_____
Temperature	_____	_____
Pulse rate	_____	_____
Breathing rate	_____	_____
Pressure	_____	_____
Weight	_____	_____
Intensity	_____	_____
Movement	_____	_____

Olfactory/Gustatory Submodalities:

Sweet	_____	_____
Sour	_____	_____
Bitter	_____	_____
Aroma	_____	_____
Fragrance	_____	_____
Pungency	_____	_____

Making good decisions means that you need to decide that you are going to get over all the difficulties that you have faced. By using submodalities, you can do a lot to change how you feel about the problems of the past and you can find yourself able to recode experiences so that what once scared you no longer does, and what once troubled you no longer affects you. You'll be learning to literally rewire your neurology so that you feel differently about your beliefs, fears, memories, relationships, and decisions.

When you begin to feel differently, you can start a new process of manifesting the kind of things you want in your life. Before you do this, it's important that you also know that once you are over your problems of what you've learned in the past, you can also get through the challenges that might face you in the present.

Part 2

GETTING THROUGH IT

Getting through things is an important part of life. We have to get over the past, but we have to get 'through' the present. There are all kinds of things that fall into this category.

People develop compulsions and habits that aren't useful. By helping them to get through these habits and behaviours, they can develop new, more useful habits, and compulsions that can help them enjoy a more wonderful life.

One of the things people sometimes have to go through is recovery. This could be recovering from a tragedy or an illness or a physical injury. Getting people to be able to get through recovery allows them to be able to get back to their full life sooner and happier.

Resignation is something that most of us feel at one stage or another in our lives. There are times when we can feel stuck and want to give up even though we know we need to continue. Once you can learn to get through these tough times, you can accomplish anything you resolve to achieve.

Of course, there are also 'big events' that happen in life. Our weddings, funerals, birthday parties, and special social events are all examples of events that require much planning and effort, and plenty of resolve. Getting through such events is an important process so that we enjoy these special moments as much as we can.

We also face 'tests' in life. Getting through exams and interviews is essential in order for us to manifest the kinds of opportunities we wish for in the future. When you can learn how to do this, it will help you create the kind of future you want and deserve.

Lastly, there are 'obligations' we feel the need to get through. From Christmas with the family to work dinners, we all have obligations that we are expected to fulfill even when we don't feel like it. In order to get through such obligations, it is necessary to discover how to control the speed of how we experience time so that we can ensure such experiences fly by.

GETTING THROUGH

Habits and Compulsions

Sometimes, we refer to our compulsions as habits and we get so used to doing something that it becomes second nature for us. Other times, compulsions can affect a person's entire life. The main difference between habits and compulsions is that habits are simply what you get used to doing and do automatically. Compulsions refer to what you feel compelled to do. There is quite an overlap between these two, so I'll cover both of them here.

Firstly, we will explore habits that people develop, such as smoking and overeating. Then, we can examine more closely the compulsions that drive people towards non-useful behaviours.

I will start by exploring how you break bad habits, because one of the things that people have to get through is a habit – they have to actually build the habit of breaking bad habits.

Over the years, one of the things that has always amazed me is that when people come into see me, they can look me straight in the eye and say that they are definitely suffering from uncertainty. I always look at them and say, *Are you sure?* and the answer is inevitably, *Yes*. Even someone who has great uncertainty always seems sure about it. There's always a place where all of these things overlap and start to self-destruct.

When somebody has a bad habit there is a first step in getting rid of it. Take something simple like cigarettes. Cigarette smoking is something where all of us who smoked at one point in time finally figure out it's just bad for us and stop. Once, I even had a doctor who smoked say that you could smoke until you're forty with no bad effects. However, I know people in their thirties who have gotten lung cancer.

It's amazing when people have bad habits, they all seem to engage in what I refer to as the 'Fudge Factor' or the 'Phenagle Phenomenon.' This is where our mind finds a way of getting out of what we know we really ought to do. Certainly, there are teenagers that smoke and may not even think about it but, eventually, all of us get to the point where we want to quit, and some people try over and over again. The problem is that without adequate mental preparation, habits can be difficult to break.

When people try and don't succeed, they build up a series of disappointments. Then they begin to build the belief that they'll never be able to succeed. The first step in breaking habits has got to be where we switch our beliefs. In the beginning of this book, we outlined the difference between good beliefs and bad beliefs, between beliefs that worked and beliefs that didn't work, between strong beliefs and weak beliefs.

Now, we're going to go back and we want to build beliefs about what's possible, so we're going to take a couple of the different techniques and lead up to it.

With smoking, for example, Step Number One is making a belief that you'll be able to quit. And your belief has to be *realistic*. Most people when they stop smoking still have a desire to smoke cigarettes occasionally. The craving comes up from time to time. Then, they become agitated. They become anxious and so they smoke a cigarette. Instead make a plan, make yourself believe that you can overcome the bad feelings that will change things. You tell yourself very simply, *I have other desires that I don't act on*. Sometimes, you just desire to lean over and smack somebody, but you don't do it. Sometimes, you just want to yell at somebody in a bank because they're taking too long, but you don't do it. We all have desires and we know enough not to act on them.

You quit smoking cigarettes, not all at once, but one cigarette at a time. We all have cravings and, a lot of them, we don't act on. I know there have been a number of times I've just wanted to beat the hell out of somebody, but I don't do it. I have strong desires I don't act on. I've seen beautiful women, stripped in their bikinis on beaches, but I don't jump on them. I can control my desires. Human beings are like that.

Think of several of these images. Again, you'll notice the submodalities. The picture is in a certain place. It's a certain size, a certain distance. It's got sound, maybe a voice that says, *You better not do this!* It comes from a certain place, and it builds a certain feeling that gets you to stop acting on your desires. Notice in which direction that feeling moves. Then take the image of cigarettes and stick it in that place.

Again, swish it over, so that you move the image into just the right place, so that you replace it with that picture of yourself, turning down cigarettes, not picking up cigarettes, doing all the things that you need to do so that you simply *don't* smoke. When I get people to quit, I don't have them throw their cigarettes out, I have them put their cigarettes in front of them. I have them light one and put it in the ashtray and stare at it, and then mentally make sure that they're able to go into the state of overcoming their desire. So that, as bad as they feel, as hard as it is to go through the withdrawal of the nicotine, for all those cravings that are there, they have control. They look at that cigarette and they struggle with it, but they still know that they cannot act on desires.

Believing Yourself a Non-Smoker

1. Think of a strong belief and elicit the submodalities. (A)
2. Think of something that you desire but you don't act upon and elicit the submodalities. (B)
3. Think of being in a situation where you had the option to smoke in the future. Move that image away and pull it up in the same submodalities of something you desire but don't act upon (B). See yourself not acting upon it and being a happy, healthy non-smoker from now on.
4. Take this image of you not acting upon the craving and being a happy, healthy non-smoker from now on and move it off into the distance and snap it back into the submodalities of the strong belief. (A)
5. Repeat steps 1–4, each time quickly.

The next thing to do is to *build* desire. Desire works in a specific way. If a person smokes and they think about cigarettes, their body would often say, *I want them!* So if you finish a meal, if you look down at a pack of cigarettes, if you see somebody else lighting a cigarette, something inside you creates desire.

In order to quit any habit, there is a way to change this desire. Let's stick with the smoking example. Stop now and make a picture of your brand of cigarettes, or what you would see if you were in a situation where you saw somebody else light up, or where you put down your fork at the dinner table and you lit up – whatever it is that would trigger your wanting to smoke a cigarette.

When you look at that image and you feel that you want a cigarette, stop and make a picture of yourself *not* smoking. See everybody else lighting up and you're *not* lighting up. When you see *that* image, adjust it, so that you look at it and you desire *that*. The trouble is most people don't realize when they look at themselves going to where they want to be, they need to see themselves inside the image. Because they're not there yet. When you look at the things that trigger bad habits, you need to see what you'd see if you were actually there. So, instead of seeing yourself smoke, you want to see the things that make you feel like you want to smoke.

Then, the trick is to swap them. Because what you need to do is change them around, whether you do it with size or you do it with distance. I like to do it with size to start with and to make a small picture where you see yourself the way you'd like to be. Make a big picture of what triggers your wanting to smoke.

Then, you take the big picture of your own pack of cigarettes, or seeing other people smoke, and you simply turn it so that it turns completely and totally white, and then take the little picture and pop it up all at once so that you tell your mind not this … this! Not cigarettes … being a non-smoker. You keep doing this, so that you take that little picture and pop it up into a big picture so that you replace the desire for cigarettes with the desire to be a non-smoker. This builds the foundation.

The truth is that if you just don't smoke for three weeks and if every time that craving comes up you put it out of your mind, it will make everything easier. It will work when you do the things that it takes to remain determined and you do the things that it takes to get through it. Getting through something isn't a one-time deal, it means that for a couple of weeks, you build a new habit.

The habit you have to build is saying to yourself powerfully, *Not cigarettes. No.* If you build this in your mind solidly enough, and you keep whiting out the images that made you crave, then every time you get that craving feeling in your body, you stop it and you spin it backwards, and then replace it with the feeling that you can control your desires.

Switching Your Craving (Swish Pattern)

1. Think about whatever trigger makes you crave something you want to stop.
2. Imagine the movie starting from this point and immediately white it out. So start the craving image and immediately white it out.
3. Replace the image immediately with an image of yourself engaging in a new behaviour, looking happy and being free. This will allow you to attach the craving to the thought of you being free from the habit.
4. Repeat steps 1–3 a few times and notice yourself feeling differently about it.

Sometimes, a habit can seem not just to be something that we do without thinking. It can feel as if we are compelled to do it as the craving seems so strong. This is where we can describe habits as compulsions. Compulsions refer to when we feel compelled to do something. People do many things compulsively. They compulsively overeat, compulsively smoke, compulsively do anything whether it is scratching their nose or pulling out their eyebrows. There are all kinds of compulsive behaviour. I've seen everything from compulsive scratchers to people who compulsively clean everything to the point where there was no way that people could live in a house with them.

This is when people have what is called obsessive compulsive disorder. This simply means that a person feels compelled to do something so much that it interferes with their ability to live a happy life.

What therapists tried to do was to look for the cause of the obsession in the hope that understanding it would help people stop. However, just like everything else, understanding by itself doesn't produce change. They were looking in the wrong place. Any compulsion doesn't function in the past, it functions in the present. To change it, you have to help people do something different in the present.

There was a woman that I treated some years ago and the odd thing about her was that, when she came to see me, she came with her husband and she began to tell me that she obsessively cleaned drawers. She opened the drawer, cleaned the drawer and then even if there would be literally nothing in it, she would look down and think that maybe there was imaginary dirt, so she would clean it again. She cleaned the toilet bowls. She vacuumed the carpets. She had little plastic foot covers so that when you walked across the carpet you didn't actually step on it.

She made her husband and her twelve-year-old son strip naked in the garage, put on disposable clothing to enter the house (including slippers like a surgeon would wear) and walk through the house so that when she looked at the house, it was never ruffled. No one could sit on the living room couch; her son could go to his room but, if there was anything out of place in the room, she would scream and yell at him to the point where her husband was ready to leave.

Now I remember looking at him and bursting out laughing and he said, *What's so funny?* and I said, *Well, let me put it this way, I can't believe that you let it get this far!* and he said, *Well, she's been seeing a psychiatrist for ten years and, you know, she's been on medication, she's done therapy ...*

I said, *Yeah, but, I have got news for you. This is your house and your son and, the fact that you've let her get away with this ... we have a name for this where I come from ... we refer to it as saying that you're just too much of a pussy to do something about it.* And he said, *Well, if I try to talk her out ...* I said, *I wasn't talking about talking. When you leave here, you're going to leave here with a bag of dirt, when you get home you're going to throw it on the carpet because if she can't deal with that, you're in big trouble!*

She looked at me and said, *If he does that, I will go insane!* I said, *Better you go insane than your son and your husband go insane, that's the way I think about it. You've got a problem, you've gotta learn to deal with it.* I asked her to close her eyes and to look at her house, and to move from room to room, and from drawer to drawer, and to see it absolutely sterile. Not a bump in the carpet, not a footprint, not a piece of underwear out of place, so that it was perfect.

As I looked at her, she sat there smiling with absolute delight on her face and I said to her, *As you look over the absolutely perfect house, I want you to realize that there is no indication of any kind that anyone lives there. In fact, a house that is this clean is a message to you that you're going to end up utterly, completely and totally alone. Your husband will leave you, your son will never talk to you, you won't have friends and, since you're such a penickety person, you won't even be able to have a cat! You'll die one of the loneliest people on the planet. But yet the empty drawer will be sterile and clean.*

She opened her eyes and looked and me, and a tear dropped from her eye. At that moment, I said, *Now, close your eyes again, and look at your carpet and see some footprints across it. Look in your son's room and see a piece of underwear on the floor and realize that what this means is that you're no longer alone. The people you love are around you. Everything that's a little out of place, a magazine turned, a page crinkled, has a different meaning to it. So if you love your son, and if you love your husband, and if you love indications that they're around you, that they haven't left you for ever, then this will make you happy. Take this feeling and begin to spin it. Because any feeling that's worth having is worth spinning and spinning and spinning.*

I got her to think differently about her house being clean so that she could see different meanings for her compulsions. Sometimes, when you get a person to see things from a different point of view, it helps them feel differently about it. I also helped her develop another quality that was absolutely essential for her to have.

This is something that is common to all problems that I help people get through. All of the examples of getting through things –

whether it's dieting, whether it's getting through dinner with relatives you don't like or whether it's going to an interview – all of us have things that we have to deal with and we can't deal with them without *determination*.

It's not going to be easy for somebody who has been this compulsive about cleaning to give it up. I can get her started by pointing out that what she believes is that it would give her comfort. Anything out of place agitated her, so like any obsessive-compulsive, she built rituals that built comfort. Whether it's locking the door six times and then unlocking it six times and then locking it six more times, all of these rituals are rituals to build comfort, as opposed to anxiety.

Anybody who has panic attacks will understand this. Some people get them if they're in a car. Some get them if they're in open spaces. Some people get panic attacks just by stepping out of their front door of their house. All of them have little rituals they engage in to make it so that they can function in the world. For example, *If I don't step on a crack on the sidewalk, then I'll be safe.* So they walk funny or they hold their hands in an odd position, whatever the ritual is that builds comfort. What they fail to realize is that it's their *mind* that creates the *dis*comfort. It's not the line on the sidewalk, it's the way you think about it.

These compulsions become *so* automated, that they're as automated as blinking when something starts to fly into your eye. Humans are learning machines. A lot of what we learn is extremely useful. We get up in the morning. We put that toothbrush in our mouth. We don't stick it in our ass because we forgot where it goes. It happens automatically, and even if you have a new toothbrush you know exactly what to do with it. You learn how these things work. This is an important part of being a person.

The problem lies when we build habits that are out of control and serve no real purpose. If you wash your hands once, they're clean. You don't need to wash them a hundred times. In order to get through these things, human beings need what I believe is one of the most important elements to get through anything: sheer, unadulterated determination. This is something you can never have enough of.

Most people fall off diets and then stop dieting because they're not determined enough. They fall off and break their diet for an hour, and they go back on it an hour later. If they break their diet at night, they just wake up in the morning and go back on it. The truth is, almost every diet works *if you stay on it*.

It requires determination to struggle through these things. The truth is, you *can* control yourself, with determination.

Become More Determined

1. Think about something you feel very determined about. Find out the submodalities for determination for you. Notice the feeling of determination and which way it spins in your body. (A)
2. Stop this and think of a habit or compulsion you want to change. Find out the submodalities of it. (B)
3. Imagine a small image of changing in the corner of this image of determination, (B) in the corner of (A).
4. In a split second, imagine this small image growing into and replacing the bigger image so that you start to see what you want to be determined to do in the same place and submodalities of

what you were determined to do. (B) replaces (A).

5. Spin the feeling of determination faster as you think about changing.
6. Repeat steps 1–5 a few times and notice yourself feeling more determined about changing this habit or compulsion.

Differences of Submodalities:	Determined	Change Behaviour
Number of images	_____	_____
Moving/Still	_____	_____
Size	_____	_____
Shape	_____	_____
Colour/Black and white	_____	_____
Focused/Defocused	_____	_____
Bright/Dim	_____	_____
Location in space	_____	_____
Bordered/Borderless	_____	_____
Flat/3D	_____	_____
Associated/Disassociated	_____	_____
Close/Distant	_____	_____

Auditory Submodalities:	Determined	Change Behaviour
Volume	_____	_____
Pitch	_____	_____
Timbre	_____	_____
Tempo	_____	_____

	Determined	Change Behaviour
Tonality	_____	_____
Duration	_____	_____
Rhythm	_____	_____
Direction of voice	_____	_____
Harmony	_____	_____

Kinesthetic Submodalities:

Location in body	_____	_____
Tactile sensations	_____	_____
Temperature	_____	_____
Pulse rate	_____	_____
Breathing rate	_____	_____
Pressure	_____	_____
Weight	_____	_____
Intensity	_____	_____
Movement	_____	_____

Olfactory/Gustatory Submodalities:

Sweet	_____	_____
Sour	_____	_____
Bitter	_____	_____
Aroma	_____	_____
Fragrance	_____	_____
Pungency	_____	_____

GETTING THROUGH

Recovery

One of the biggest examples of something that people have to get through is recovering from an operation. This also covers recovering from a stroke, recovering from physical damage or car accidents. It can seem very difficult because it's discouraging that after you are through whatever medical procedures that saved your life, you must go through the experience of rehabilitation.

The art of getting through things is about being able to have determination. It's also about being able to have the right beliefs. Many people never really recover from things that they actually could. There are very good reasons for this. One is they listen to the wrong experts. I have always been amazed by this, not just by medical doctors but by nurses, relatives, many people trying to help you are all telling you that you are never going to be able to recover fully.

When I was in the hospital after I had a stroke some years ago, I was taken to the emergency ward. There was a medical doctor and as I was taken off towards surgery. He put a hand on either side of my face and said to me, *Can you hear me?* I remember looking up at him and he was blurry to me as the sedatives were settling in. I said, *Yes* and he said, *No matter what anyone says to you, no matter who they are, I am telling you, you can make a full recovery.*

It stuck in my mind because it wasn't more than a few days later – with tubes coming out of my arms, with painkillers drilling through my body – that the first person came to me and told me that I had had a stroke and that the stroke would paralyse me for the rest of my life. Then, I heard what the doctor had said to me, *No matter what anyone says to you, you can make a full recovery.*

The truth is it happens all the time. Even with the worst strokes, they can't explain why some people recover and some don't. I know that when it happens to you, it seems overwhelming and impossible, like you will never be whole again, but this is the time to build up a big belief in what you can do. Remember doctors, psychiatrists, nurses or your relatives are not psychic. They can't predict the future. No one can tell you what you can't do.

People can tell you what they think but they can't really predict what's possible and impossible. There are cases of spontaneous remission, where people for no reason under the sun, just get well. There are filing cabinets full of cases of spontaneous remission. I discovered the trick to what helped me to have a full physical recovery. Whether they decided I was never going to be able to walk again, I decided I was going to be able to walk. I would focus every fibre in my soul in being able to first move my toes and then my feet and then my knees, and then being able to stand and then being able to walk.

It requires that you push yourself harder than anyone else. This also means that you have to be insulated from disappointment. Disappointment always requires adequate planning and it's always added to if you have help from others.

People look at you and say, *Don't be discouraged, don't be disappointed, don't be frustrated.* The unconscious part of your mind doesn't process negation so, of course, it's like saying, *Don't think of blue.* Immediately, you think of blue, so it's always useful to have a part of you that abreacts.

Abreaction is about having a polarity response. The more people tell you that you can't do something, the more you want to do it. How do you build this into yourself? You build desire in the right direction.

When it's time to get yourself to stick to an exercise program, let alone a recovery program, this is the time when you want absolutely, overwhelming determination and resolve that turns itself into behavior. So that the more things get difficult, the more you apply yourself. Most of the great minds I have met had this built into them when they were young.

I know this is true of myself in my own work. Everything I succeeded at, I had people telling me it couldn't be done. It's amazing how many people were able to predict that I wouldn't be able to find a way of getting people through phobias. They would predict that I would not be able to find a way to help schizophrenics.

I had psychiatrist after psychiatrist, psychologist after psychologist, all these people who themselves couldn't do it, telling me that I wouldn't be able to take my new approaches, my new skills, my new methodology and be able to help people. They were telling me this when they themselves didn't even know which person I was going to work with.

These were people who I referred to as the *prophets of doom*. These were the people who said not to try as hard as you possibly could. If you say you tried to open a door, it means you didn't really open it, but if you tried with every fibre of your soul, you would be surprised what you could do. When you become fully determined and when you only measure the degree of success that you get, you would be amazed at what's possible.

When I lay in that hospital bed, as soon as I got one toe to move, I thought, *I can move the other toe.* I moved on to the foot and began to move the foot. The same is true about solving every single difficulty. The problem is that if you measure where you are not, then you say, *It's time to feel failure.* However, on the other hand, if you only measure what you are succeeding at, it starts to work.

You have a little feeling in your leg, then you have more feeling. If you figure out how much better you are today than you were yesterday and you keep doing it each day then, little by little, you push yourself through whatever experience you're going through. The truth is that if you're going down one long road and you make just the smallest turn, you actually get further from where you would have been. Eventually, two weeks down the road you are in a completely different state than you would have been in if you had kept going straight.

The truth is that the way you get through things is by building resolve. I know that you, at some time, have resolved to do something that seemed impossible. When kids learn to ride a bicycle, it seems that they will never be able to do it. Then, mysteriously, they learn a little of this, a little of that, a little of how to steer, a little of how to balance. They use training wheels, whatever it takes. Eventually, down the road, all of these things are put into the behaviour of riding a bike.

Whether it's learning to play an instrument, learning to write with a pencil, learning to type on a keyboard, all of us have been so determined because we have wanted something so bad that we were able to get through that stage where it was awkward and find the resolve that kept us doing it until we got where we wanted to go.

If you go back in your memory and find this powerful example where you were resolved, this is the beginning. It may be back in your childhood. If you think about something and think about what it was like at the time – see what you saw when you were there, hear what you heard and feel what you felt – you'll be able to bring back the feeling of resolve. If you remember struggling through it and failing at it and getting back on and doing it again until you succeeded, it will help you greatly. This is an important part of learning.

All children do it. They stand up and they fall down. They stand up and they fall down, but they keep standing up till they get to the part where they can walk, where they can run. That ability doesn't disappear because you have a stroke or because you are older. Having resolve is what gets you through the really hard stuff.

Resolve to Recover

1. Imagine yourself fully recovered. See what you would see, hear what you'd hear, feel how good you would feel. Really imagine it vividly.
2. Recall any bad suggestion that anyone gave you about not recovering and hear them say it is a voice that you do not trust or believe.
3. Promise yourself in a certain tone of voice that you will recover fully.
4. Remember all the times you got through tough situations and you were a better person as a result of it. Remember how it felt to be determined enough to get through anything. See what you saw, hear what you heard, feel what you felt.
5. Spin this feeling as you promise yourself again with this determined feeling and imagine yourself getting through it, recovering and each time you feel like giving up spinning this feeling even stronger.
6. Imagine yourself continually focused on getting better and enjoying the challenge of recovering and dealing with the tough times and situations with this spinning feeling of determination and resolve.

GETTING THROUGH

Resignation

There are certain times in life when all we feel like doing is resigning to fate and giving up. Maybe it's because we're tired of something not working, maybe it's because we can't seem to find a way through, maybe we get bored or distracted, or maybe we get heartbroken. For whatever reason, there are times when we no longer have the will to go on or the energy to finish something.

Getting through resignation means learning how you can get through the tough times and become better for it. This comes down again to manifesting this really important quality: resolve.

Resolve is what gets us through the difficult things we all have to deal with. It's what gets you through the hard funeral and all the people feeling sorry for you, so that you can deal with your own grief and get on with your life. It is what makes a diet work. So that when you plan your diet, you resolve to stay on it and resolve that, if you fall off it, you get right back on it again. This is just like you did with that bicycle when you were a kid, just like you did when you learned to walk, just like you did when you learned to speak a language.

The number of people who give up learning a language is astronomical. It's a multibillion dollar industry and most of the people who listen to a language CD or go to a language class give up. The fact that it's difficult doesn't make them more propelled to continue.

What you need to do in your mind is set up a system where you go along with all of your resolve and plan to have difficulties. Most people plan for it to be too easy. Instead, plan to fall off your diet. Plan to struggle and have trouble learning the words. Then plan that when that happens to go back to the beginning and double the amount of determination you have. The trick is to look into the future and say, *I am going to fall off my diet ten times and each time I fall off it I am going to become more determined to get back on it and do it even more.*

Getting On and Getting Back On

1. Think of something that you want to be motivated and disciplined to do, for example going on and sticking to a diet.
2. Think of how much you want to be healthy and fit and develop your ideal body by dieting. Really imagine it in vivid detail until you feel really motivated and determined to go on this diet. Amplify the feeling by spinning it faster.
3. Imagine yourself going on the diet as you spin this feeling. Then imagine yourself falling off it at some point in the future and spin the feeling faster as you imagine yourself getting straight back on.

105

4. Imagine being on the diet and falling off and then bring the feeling of determination back again and spin it as you imagine going straight back on the diet again.

If you miss a day of exercise, you have to become even more determined so that you try even harder. Failure means you stop. That is what failure is by definition. Failure means you stop doing the activity. Failure is an artificial determination of time.

When people say, *I failed to finish my book*, it is because they stopped. It is not because the world has ended. All they have to do is go back and be more determined to apply themselves more. It doesn't require that you increase the amount of frustration you have. It requires that you forget about your frustration. Every failure is something that you should ignore and every failure should mean you should try even more.

The more you don't do it, the more you apply yourself. That's how all great people succeed. When I studied great athletes, one of the things that amazed me was what they would say to me. It's the same thing that great musicians and concert pianists told me. When you would say to them, *You are so fabulous*, they would look at me and say, *Not really. I could be better*, because they always believed they could be better so they kept getting better. When they did things that were a little bit off, they did a little bit more. They kept at it. They had that spirit.

When I studied a close-up magician, he had one of the best strategies I had ever seen. When he wanted to learn a card trick, he would turn it around and see what it would look like from the outside. He would see all the separate movements you would have to do to create the illusion.

He then ran the movie in his mind and stuck his hands inside it and tried to keep up. He did this and to the extent that he matched the movie, he got a good feeling. The minute he fell behind, he would stop and start over. He became addicted to the good feeling of success. That is what real determination is. It is about amplifying good feeling from being in the process.

It's not that you get to the end and feel good. It's the process of feeling that the more you get in the right direction, the better you feel. The fact is that once you succeed in something, it is over. It's not that you get to feel good at the end. So, if it feels bad to practice things or if it feels bad to diet or to exercise, then you're not doing it right.

You need to go back, create a good feeling, spin it in your body and then apply the activity. The more you do it, the more you spin the feeling. Taking control of what feels good is an important part of serious determination. It's what gets you through things and getting through things will make life loads better.

GETTING THROUGH
Big Events

There are some major events that you have to plan that have all kinds of details that you need to be aware of. An example of one of these is a wedding, where you have to have a dress, a cake, bridesmaids, groomsmen, and a million other little things which all must be accounted for on the day. Often, these events also involve you being dependent on other people – like the best man – to show up and be in the right state. In many ways, events like these start out like any business. You need to have good selection and recruiting.

The big mistake that people make is that they choose somebody through peer pressure rather than choose somebody who is qualified. It doesn't matter what the task is. If you're going to hire a caterer, you want to make sure that they know how to cater and that they do things on time. You want to talk to people to make sure they do a good job so that they don't screw you up. You don't want to hire a band that's notoriously late. You need to get yourself to that step of getting yourself to be reassured. Otherwise, you'll spend the time worrying about everything that can go wrong as a way of trying to avoid it. It's much better if you sit down and figure out all the qualities of each step that has to go well and figure out what it would take to get it that way in the first place rather than just hoping that it's all going to work out.

It's a big mistake to pick somebody *just* because they're your friend. You have to make sure your friend knows how to do the things they need to do. You need to know that they're not somebody who is going to argue with you about everything. When people are planning big events, one of the mistakes they make is not to realize that they should just make the decisions about what they want. They should read all the magazines they want and talk to everybody they want to. Then, they can make a decision about what they want instead of re-deciding and re-deciding because somebody else comes along and says, *You could have done this!*

If you want to get through something, you have to decide how you delegate time. You decide, *This amount of time is planning, this amount of time is doing and this is the event.* It is true that you could always do things better. I wrote a book with somebody once and every time we finished, they would go back and say, *We could make this better.* Of course, that's always true. However, after two years of revising this book six or seven times, it wasn't even the same book. We could have written three volumes on the subject and instead we kept revising the one volume so that it became the third volume instead of getting it done and getting it out.

I finally just handed it to the person and said, *I'm done* and he said, *We could make it better* and I said, *No. You could make it better. I'm going to write my own books instead.* If people keep on revising things over and over again, all it does is create stress. What you need to do is to say, *OK. I'm going to spend a month making these decisions. Then I'm going to spend two months getting this stuff done. Then I'm going to relax.* That is also one of the things that you have to plan on. If you don't plan on feeling good and being certain about things, then it won't necessarily happen.

In this book, you've been learning about the difference between good decisions and bad decisions. Once you make good decisions, what makes them work is sticking to them until you're done. You can always plan another event later on. You could get married once a year if you wanted to. There are no rules about that. When you're going to plan a big wedding, if you suffer for five months to make one good day, it's not a bargain.

You should set aside the time it takes to do it well. Just do it well and the rest of the time forget about it. If you find your mind is winding around things, making you feel bad, then you've got to unwind them the other way. This is not just true for weddings. It is true for every big event that we organize in life. If you plan cleverly, and you plan on feeling good during the process, that will allow you to get through the challenges much more effectively.

Big Occasion Tips

1. Plan how much time you are going to spend on each part of the preparation and process.
2. Give yourself time for deciding things, doing the tasks that need to be done, picking the people to delegate some tasks to and being able to relax and look forward to the event.

3. Decide on criteria for the different assistants for the event. Ensure that each assistant fulfils the criteria for their role.
4. Accept that the event will never be *perfect*, so the idea is to make it as good as you can. Plan for challenges happening along the way and imagine yourself handling them easily. Make decisions and then stick to them.
5. Imagine everything working out through each phase and the event going ahead wonderfully.

GETTING THROUGH

Tests (Exams and Interviews)

The trick to getting through tests is adequate preparation. With any tests, from exams to interviews, to a certain degree you can prepare what it is that you're supposed to talk or write about. You can imagine going through it but, when you do imagine going through it, you'll also have to imagine going through it in the right state. The thing about being interviewed is that people are not just looking for the right answers, they're looking for the right kind of person. If you imagine yourself being nervous or fidgeting, or your voice cracking, or making big mistakes, and you run through every wrong thing that you could do in your mind then, when you get in there, you'll be more apt to do them.

If people are looking for problems, they have a tendency to find them. On the other hand, if you can imagine what would be the perfect state to be in, that will work much better for you. What would you look like in the perfect state? What would you sound like at your

112

most confident? What would your voice be like when you are at your best? Answer these questions and literally practice matching the picture in your mind and make it so that you know what it feels like. Once you do this, you'll start to feel differently. You do it before you walk in and not after you get there because, by then, it's way too late. Before you get out of your car, you put yourself in that wonderful state and spin that set of feelings of you at your best so that the closer you get to the door the more you feel confident and ready.

You can even practice this before you get there. Imagine getting into your car and going into the right state. Imagine getting out of the car and every step you take, you spin the feeling faster and you make the feeling stronger so that you're in the right state when you're in the right place. Most people get into the right place and go into the wrong state and then try and fight their way back there and, by the time they get there, it's over and they've lost their opportunity. The trick is to be able to plan to be going where you want and the closer you get to what you want, the more you're in a state that's going to work for you. This is so that you can answer the best answers and so that you can make the best presentation you can make.

People aren't just listening to what you say. They're also looking at what you do and how you come across. The more competitive the position, the more that this is true. Of course, you should be prepared for things like reading up on particular kind of information. You should also stay in the right state while you're reading up on it. Avoid reading up in desperation and then expecting to be in the right state when you remember it.

Doing an Excellent Interview

1. Think of a time where you felt confident and focused. See what you saw at the time, hear what you heard. Feel how confident and good you felt and amplify the feeling by spinning it faster.

2. Imagine yourself going to the interview and arriving at it spinning the confident feeling and imagine that feeling amplifying as you walk in the door and meet the interviewers.

3. Imagine being in the interview and stand or sit as you will be in the interview. Imagine being asked each question, spin the feeling as you respond with confidence and this feeling keeps spinning.

4. Imagine you get asked a question you weren't expecting but as you keep that feeling spinning you respond with confidence and clarity in the moment.

5. Run right through this process over and over again and when it is time to go to the interview, you will find yourself feeling really confident about it.

All learning is state conditioned. This is why people have trouble with exams. They study and they're calm and then they go in and they're nervous in the tests. They can't get to the answers because the answers are associated with the calm state. So either be nervous when you study and be nervous when you take the test, or else be calm when you study and make sure you're calm when you take the test.

Go inside your mind and imagine going back into the room that you studied in. See the walls and feel the furniture so that you put yourself back in the same state as you were in at that time. Then look at the paper and start answering the questions. Human beings have the unique quality of being able to create their reality internally and then to superimpose it on the outside. If you've no control over that, some people call that schizophrenia. If you do have control over it, then you're a creative genius. I recommend the latter.

This means being able to use your imagination to internally remember what you need to remember. Your own ability to go inside your mind and make images and run movies gives you a wonderful resource with which to store time. To help people get through exams I like to teach them how to cheat internally.

Instead of having notes or information on the outside, I have people vividly study some notes and practice imagining those notes on locations in the room. I have them practise hallucinating notes everywhere so that, when they go into the exam, they can hallucinate the notes they've studied in front of them and have that information available to them.

Getting Through Exams

1. Before you study, organize your study so that you make it similar to the kinds of circumstances you'll face in the exams.
2. Remember a time you felt confident, excited, and superbly focused. See what you saw, hear what you heard, and feel how you felt. Amplify the feeling.
3. As you study take time to look at particular notes you have and practice hallucinating them in different locations around the room. Do so until you can see them anywhere you put them by imaging them vividly.

4. When you go into the exam, bring about the same state of confidence, excitement and superb focus again and spin the feeling.
5. Begin to answer each question but imagine being back in your room and hallucinate the answers in front of you in the same way.
6. See yourself vividly and notice the way you are smiling, breathing, standing, and moving. Move in that way.

GETTING THROUGH
Obligations

As human beings, we are constantly faced with having to endure things which, in themselves, are not necessarily bad or good but for some people can seem unpleasant. Sometimes, going over to a relative's house and having Christmas dinner can seem like the most excruciating thing in the world. Having to sit through an opera could be a torturous event that would seem like it lasted for hours. I can remember standing in line at the bank and I thought I had been there for two hours and I was really only there for ten minutes. Some people make things a lot worse than they need to be. The trick to this is to have adequate preparation.

People usually think about how horrible or how unpleasant a future event is going to be. They plan for it. It doesn't matter if it's a test at school or sitting through a school play. Whatever the event is, people can make things worse or better by how they think about it in advance in their mind. Events themselves are not necessarily good or bad. Our response to them is good or bad.

People will go to a party. They'll be there for four hours and it feels like it goes by in two minutes. The world doesn't actually spin any faster. It just feels that way because we're in a good state. If you think about the things that make an excruciating event *excruciating* and you feel bad while you do it, and you do it over and over in preparation for the event, when you get there, it will be even worse.

I've always said that disappointment requires adequate planning. So does suffering. Suffering requires adequate planning because you have to know which bad feeling to have and when to have it. When Uncle Fred goes off on an unending story, you know it's time to pull your hair out by the roots. Instead, if you can learn to focus on only what it is that you enjoy, then you can start to make the things, which seem unpleasant, silly.

You can do this through using a model like submodalities. What one person finds silly and what another person finds excruciating can be identical. The truth is that it works much better when you take adequate preparation for the things that you have to go through. Whether you have to go through a long and boring day in court or a deposition or all kinds of things, you can plan to deal with it more effectively.

In preparation for it, you go through and run the movie inside your mind and while you're running it you make it silly. Make it so that it doesn't bother you. It's silly that the same things can, year in year out, have driven you crazy since you know that they're going to happen. You should be able to feel differently and if you don't, then you can count on the fact that you'll suffer like you always do.

There are a couple of mental tricks that are really important to how you do this. In order to make time move faster, human beings mentally do something different. For example, one of the things you do is that when you're driving down the road and things are moving very fast in your peripheral vision versus the centre of your vision, you always go into states of time distortion. That's why when people drive really fast down the road and then they change speeds, they're still moving fast at about thirty or forty miles per hour, yet they feel like they are crawling because they were going seventy miles an hour beforehand. It takes a while for the brain to adjust.

When you want time to go faster, you need to go inside your head and not just run a movie of what's going to happen so that you know when to be disappointed, or when to be in a state of frustration, or a state where you feel like pulling your hair out. You need to run it so that what you see in the centre of the image moves very, very slowly and everything on the sides moves very fast.

For example, when Uncle Fred is telling that same old, long, boring story, you can watch everybody move around like they're Charlie Chaplin figures, so that you plan in your head to make it so that it goes by quickly. It's about having adequate mental preparation so that, when it occurs, you go into a time warp so that it doesn't seem like it takes hours. In fact, the trick is to run the centre of the image in your mind really slowly so that Uncle Fred talks at half the speed he normally does but everything else moves really fast. Then, when the event actually occurs and he's actually talking faster than you had him talking in your head, it's going to seem easier.

Instead of wishing he would do things more quickly and imagining how fast it could be, you'll be doing the opposite. When it feels like it's slow, you make it so that you imagine it going ten times slower than it normally does, so that when it occurs in reality, it feels faster.

This is to do with contrast and you can create the kind of contrast you want in your mind. Time is a very relative thing for human beings. Sometimes, time appears to move very fast and, sometimes, it seems to go by very slowly.

A big part of this is how we go into the situation and how we make a distinction in the receptors in our eyes. Our eyes have a part known as the fovea centralis, which is like a central vision detector that detects shape; we have movement detectors for peripheral vision. When you make big distinctions internally between those things, you can set yourself up to change your perceptions because when we practice driving at first, everything is overwhelming, it's all moving too fast but, as we get used to it, we sort this out in our mind so that we can drive very fast and it doesn't feel fast.

Jet pilots flying at twice the speed of sound really have to do this. Can you imagine what it's like to fly at twice the speed of sound and then get off and ride on a golf cart back to the terminal? They must feel as if they're going two inches an hour because their mind is set up for it. It's a mental trick to be able to shift from one event to another, from one time to another.

Speeding Up Time

1. Think of a situation where you would like time to go by quickly.
2. Imagine the situation happening and whatever it is that is happening that makes it seem like time drags, see that event happening in front of you going really slowly.
3. Imagine everything else around you is going really quickly and flying by like in a Charlie Chaplin movie. For example, if it involves

talking to someone, you will see them in the centre of the movie talking really slowly while the rest of the background of the movie all runs around very quickly.

4. Continue to see the event go slowly while everything in your peripheral vision moves really quickly.

5. When you actually arrive and begin the event whether it is standing in a line or talking to someone or watching something, you will find it goes by far more quickly than you expected.

6. You can also go through this process while you are experiencing the event and it works just as effectively.

There are also things you can do if you want time to move in the other direction. Sometimes, it's a good idea to make time move more slowly. You can do exactly the opposite and practicing making some things seem fast and making some things feel like they are going by far more slowly. You can also make things more funny and make things more serious. These are all distinctions that can be made with the model of submodalities because when you use the model of submodalities, you can do a lot.

You can look at the things you really enjoy and you can look at the things that you have to do because they are socially required of you – and notice the differences. I remember going to parent–teacher nights for my children and listening to a second grade teacher explain to me how things were made with construction paper. It would have been very easy to pull my hair out but that's the time when you want to be able to grab a hold of the time throttle and speed things up, so that you're imaging things moving slower than they actually are.

The reason things are excruciating is because people in their mind think that it could be going by faster and they imagine it going by faster; when it's not, they feel the disjointed nature of it. When you realize somebody could be telling you something ten times faster than they are, then of course it seems even slower. However, if you imagined it coming out even half a syllable at a time in slow motion then they'll seem like they're going faster. The more that you create disparity in time deliberately in the right direction, the more that it'll work for you.

Handling Christmas Dinner

1. Practice speeding up time by imagining the parts of Christmas dinner you don't enjoy happening in the way described above.
2. Plan to make the most of the parts that you do enjoy. Focus on what you can do to enjoy the whole experience even more.
3. Consider the kinds of things that different people will say and do during the course of the dinner and decide on the best way to respond to them.
4. If necessary, you can take an image of the person saying something and change the submodalities of the image so that they are in a small, black and white image off in the distance with a clown's nose on their face to make you feel less affected by them.
5. Think of a time where you felt really good and manifest that feeling and imagine going right through Christmas dinner as you feel the feeling.
6. Remember why you are at the Christmas dinner and do what you can to improve your relationship and feelings with everyone at the table.

There are many different obligations that we have to get through in life that we aren't always looking forward to at the time. When you can begin to learn how to get through different events and problems, there is one more element that is important in moving on to a better life.

This is how you can start to get *to* things. Once you begin to learn how to build determination, resolve and a new belief that you will get through anything, you are well on your way towards dealing with the tricky situations of the present. When you add to this adequate mental preparation and your own ability to control your perception of time and your responses to things, you'll find yourself being able to get through anything. You will also be able to look forward to the future and begin to focus on all those things that you enjoy.

Part 3

GETTING TO IT

Being able to get to things is the important third section of this book. It means getting to the point where you do your taxes, where you have some fun, where you get around to actually having sex, you get around to meeting people, making more money or doing exercise. It's about getting to do all the exercises that are actually in this book.

Most people I've found in life spend far too much time worrying about their problems and not enough time getting to have fun. I always like to ask people, *Once you have gotten over your problems, what are you going to do with all that spare time?* Getting to have more fun is an important part of being happy.

Another part of being happy is making sure that you have good relationships. There are many people that spend their lives slaving away and fail to focus on the important things in life. Getting to love means being able to spend quality time with your family and making time for that special someone in your life.

In order to find someone that you love, or even build up a better social network and group of friends, it's important to get to meet more people. There are billions of people on this planet so there's no reason why any one of us should ever have to feel lonely. Learning to like yourself, improving how you feel around others as well as knowing how to flirt are some of the good things to know in getting to meet people.

Getting to important duties is something that we all need to do. Whether it's taxes or studying, there are some things that just need to happen for us to be able to do well in our lives. Being able to motivate yourself to do them is a useful skill to have.

For example, getting to exercise is one of those important tasks that can have great benefits in your life. If you can learn to feel motivated to do it constantly, you'll find it a lot easier to become fitter and healthier.

When you do turn your attention to the rest of your life, it is, of course, important to be able to organize things more effectively. Once you begin to plan and arrange your life, you'll free up more time to be able to do the other things you want to do.

Some things don't require as much motivation but do require know-how. Making more money is something that can help you out quite a lot. If you can just learn a few simple tricks, you can find out how to increase how much you make.

Finally, I will talk about making big decisions. Because there is so much choice out there, people often come to me who have trouble in deciding what to do with their life. Once you can get to make those decisions, you can begin to manifest the kind of life you want.

GETTING TO
Fun

One of the things I find people have trouble doing most is actually having fun. The truth is that human beings do the strangest things to have fun. Some people jump out of perfectly good aeroplanes for fun when the planes are not even broken. Some people even drag string through the water for fun.

There are numerous games where people whack balls around from here to there. They use sticks and hit balls into little holes. They take big balls and throw them into small holes. They take oblong balls and chase them while they bounce, all in the name of fun. People play cards and do all kinds of things that are not intrinsically interesting but human beings have the capability to not only make things interesting but also fun.

Wouldn't it be nice if you could make things, which didn't seem like fun, feel a lot more enjoyable? Again, this is one of the things that you can learn to do. Paying attention to things and getting better at something is where we are really good. If you take something you actually really enjoy and something you really struggle with, then the submodalities will be different. By definition, so will the feelings.

You can look at something you enjoy and amplify it. You can make it so that you not only enjoy it but also the feelings associated with it get stronger. This can be done easily by the process of amplification. This means that you take the image of the thing you enjoy in your mind and, when you look at it, if you feel drawn towards it, then you double the size of the picture. You turn up the brightness and you speed up the image. You adjust the sounds so that the feelings get stronger.

Once they are strong enough, you literally spin them faster and you even them up so that they are centred on your midline, the middle of your body. You make it so that they go all the way down to your toes and all the way up to the top of your head and down through your nose. You imagine all of this vividly.

The faster you spin it, the stronger your feelings get. Then, as you do this, you pull up the thing that you want to be more motivated to do, the thing you want to be fun, the thing you want to get to, and get to soon.

Making Things Fun

1. Think of something that you enjoy doing a lot. Notice the submodalities.
2. Go through and amplify the feelings of enjoyment. Do this by playing around with the submodalities and adjusting them so that the feelings get stronger and more intense.

3. Spin the feelings throughout your body and keep increasing them. Then imagine something that you want to enjoy more and think of it vividly as you keep spinning the feeling faster and faster throughout your body.

There are many things which, in and of themselves, are fun and, for some reason, humans have trouble getting started. One of those things, of course, is sex. It always amazes me that couples don't look at each other and say, *Let's go in the other room and have sex*. They will lie in bed and think about it and neither one of them will say a word. Psychologists will look at this and come up with reasons why. They will explain how they are afraid of failure and have the fear of rejection. They will use every excuse under the sun. The truth is they simply are not motivated enough.

People spend far too much time having long, meaningful arguments in bed and not nearly enough time enjoying themselves with each other. If they went inside and spun the desired state faster and faster and just smiled at their partner and asked them, things would work much better. Sometimes, you will get a *Yes*. Sometimes you will get a *No*. The more you ask, the more opportunities there will be to get an answer. The more you keep this in mind, the more you will enjoy yourself.

Better Sex

1. Think of your loved one.
2. Remember the time they were at their sexiest and you felt most attracted to them.

3. See what you saw, hear what you heard, and feel what you felt. Notice the feeling of lust and spin it right through you faster and faster.
4. Smile at them and seduce them. Aim to make them feel as good as they possibly can. Recall every amazing experience you have had with them and spin the feelings as you are with them.

GETTING TO

Love

It strikes me as very odd that people put off things like expressing their love to their loved ones. For example, often people put off things like spending time with their kids. They always tell me, *I don't have enough time*, but yet the amount of time they spend worrying about things that they can't do anything about is huge. There are, in fact, things that they could actually do something about that they would enjoy.

People need to prioritize. They need to allocate sufficient time for their journey to work, but they won't allocate time to how long they're going to spend thinking about work. If you decide, *Well, I've got to drive to work, it's going to take me an hour, so I might as well spend that hour thinking about what I'm going to do when I get there*, then you will free up more time. In the hour or so before you leave the house, you can actually talk to your children rather than running through your mind all the stuff you're going to do that day.

People talk about *time* management but they don't talk about *mental* management. Mental management is what produces productive human beings. Productive people decide, *I'm going to spend this time doing this and I'm going to put my full attention to it. When I come home from work, I'm going to give my full attention to my wife, and then I'm going to give my full attention to my kids, and then to my dog. Then I'm going to devote an hour to spending my full attention on something else.* This is for everything from watching TV to pondering some work issues. Then, you attend fully to talking to your wife, or sleeping, or whatever the task is.

Some people lay down to sleep and instead they senselessly ruminate over what they didn't do during the day, and then they complain to me that they are insomniacs. The truth is they are not really insomniacs, they're being stupid. They don't plan their day out. If you're going to worry, at least decide when you're going to do it.

People also say that they can't stop thinking about something. That's not true, you actually can. You can by thinking about something else, and by setting time limits. If you can wake yourself up out of a sound sleep at a certain time and turn your alarm off just before it beeps, you should be able to wake yourself out of the stupor of life and stop worrying. You should be able to tell your husband or wife that you love them and say hello to your kids.

You need to look at your husband or wife and listen to whatever they talk about. It doesn't have to be important. What's important is that you listen to them. That's all that matters. The rest of it really doesn't make any difference. You look them in the eye and you smile and look at their face, and realize that you're one of the lucky people who is not utterly and totally alone and miserable.

It's also important that you get to remind yourself of how lucky you are. I talked earlier in the book about how you can help yourself fall out of love with someone. You can also practice falling more and more in love with someone by doing the opposite process.

When people are in love they associate with all the good memories and if people do something that upsets them, they see themselves in that memory. If you want to stay in love, which is an important process not to be undermined, the best thing to do is to be able to make sure that you associate with good memories.

Also, anything unpleasant – when they dropped your favourite glass or knocked over and cracked your favourite picture or spilled something on your favourite dress – you see yourself in those memories and push them off into the distance. You take every single good memory you have from the day you met this person and bring it close like it's happening now, so it seems like just yesterday that you met, just yesterday that you fell in love.

Falling More in Love

1. Think of your loved one.
2. Remember the first time that you felt in love with them. Imagine it like it was yesterday. See what you saw, hear what you heard, feel how good you felt. Spin the feelings of love right through your body.
3. Think of anything that bothers you about their behaviour and disassociate yourself from the behaviour and memories so that you are looking at your loved one from a distance.
4. Immediately bring up all the memories of times where you loved being with them and step into those memories and associate into

them so you are seeing and experiencing what you saw and feeling what you felt at the time.

5. Run through all of these wonderful experiences and amplify the feeling of love and spin it throughout your body. Then look at them and notice yourself feeling like you did the first time you fell for them.

Once you are feeling even more in love with them, you also need to do certain things differently. You need to get to say the things that you're not saying. Maybe, you don't tell your husband you love him. You don't tell your wife you love her. You don't compliment your children on the things they do well. Maybe, you've got too much of a temper. Maybe, you get angry too often and you haven't gotten around to doing something about it. What it boils down to is that you have to first make a decision that you're going to change something. You can do this by noticing the qualities of decisions that you followed through on. Then you decide to tell your loved ones that you love them and you place that decision in the same qualities of decisions that you follow through on.

Make a Decision to Follow Through

1. Think of a time you made a really good decision that you followed through on, (A).
2. Elicit the submodalities.
3. Think of a decision that you want to make. For example, telling your loved ones you love them, (B).
4. Elicit the submodalities.

5. In a quick motion send the image of the decision that you want to make (B) way out into the distance and bring it back up in the position and submodalities of the decision you followed through on (A).
6. Repeat until you know that you will make this decision and follow through on it.

Once you've decided and you have a good solid decision that you can live by, then make yourself believe that you're going to do it. Then you go about switching your feelings. You create the kinds of feelings that you want.

Make feelings of being tolerant and spin them inside your body. Then think of all the things that your children have done that have aggravated you and make them life size, and look at the same thing that aggravated you but spin the feeling of being patient. And then slowly, over time, you'll find that you get around to acting differently when the circumstances arise. If you wait, you'll wait and wait, and then you'll look back and regret, but if you look forward and plan and plan and plan, then you can do something about it.

Become More Tolerant

1. Think of a time where you felt really tolerant and patient. Notice the feeling, which direction it spins in, and spin it throughout your whole body.
2. Think of something that you want to be more tolerant of and patient of in the future.
3. Spin the feeling of tolerance as you imagine waiting for and doing this activity.

4. Repeat this with different examples until you feel more tolearnt about all of the experiences.

Getting to love more means actually practicing what love is. Often we talk about love as being a thing that exists but it's important to remember that love is also a verb. Love is what we do, so in order to get to more love we need to do it more often. This means practicing being patient, tolerant, and in love with the most important people in our lives and making them a priority that we can enjoy every second with them.

Tips for More Love in Your Life

1. Make time for your loved ones and make it time that you spend fully thinking about them.
2. Be more patient and tolerant with them.
3. Regularly, remember vividly the times you were most in love with your partner and amplify the memories.
4. Say the things you want to say to them and do it regularly.
5. Do your best to make sure every moment you spend together is a wonderful and fun moment.
6. Perform a random act of kindness. Be extra nice to someone you don't know or make a stranger smile at least once a day.

GETTING TO
Meet People

Another thing that people seem to have a problem doing is meeting people. It's fascinating how many people there are on the planet and yet there are so many people that just don't approach others.

Teresa hired me as a consultant. She worked at a large company. She was an executive and she came to me and said that she wanted to be able to go to a big company party where there would be lots of people who could be good connections worldwide. However, she was afraid to go to the party and believed that if she went there she wouldn't speak to anybody. She explained that she'd always been, to an extent, socially phobic.

Not to the degree that she couldn't go out in public or talk to people but that whenever she was in a social situation rather than being people's boss, she'd feel totally uncomfortable and would stutter and stammer if she spoke at all. She told me that, if she could just go to this one party and enjoy herself, she would be able to make connections that would help her to get promoted and all kinds of things. I asked her, *What is it going to take for you to be able to get to the party number one, and number two to get through the party and enjoy yourself?* Those are two different things because, typically, she had avoided these situations. The first thing I did was to make her think of something she desired immensely.

It doesn't even matter what she picked. In her case, she wanted a Jaguar. A brand new car – not the cat! She remembered when she had seen the Jaguar, the one that looks like an Aston Martin, she had decided then that was the car for her. She'd been saving money for the down payment and had figured out how to sell her current car. Also, she had planned the financing and was going through all the steps to buy her new car. She was taking delivery of it the following week. When I asked her about it, you could see the twinkle in her eye. Her whole physiology changed.

I had her close her eyes, think about the car that she wanted and spin up the feeling so that it spun faster and faster and then I had her turn and replace the Jaguar with a picture of her at this party, being socially adept, talking to people, giggling, and telling jokes. I had her imagine walking up and introducing herself to others, and asked her if she really desired to be that way.

Become More Motivated

1. Think of a big image of something that you crave or that really motivates you. Notice the submodalities.
2. In the corner of this image, imagine a small image of what you want to be motivated to do.

3. In a split second, imagine this small image growing into and replacing the bigger image, so that you start to see what you want to be motivated to do in the same place and submodalities of what you craved.

4. Repeat steps 1–3 a few times and notice yourself feeling the motivating feelings for the new behaviour.

Of course, spinning the desire, looking at herself being able to do things she thought were impossible she said, *Oh, I'd love to be that way.* So I said, *But do you want it?* She told me she did. I said, *OK, all we need to do is to have a plan. Now that you can desire to go to the party, we have to be able to get you there and have you feel differently the whole time. In order to be socially adept, you have to be at ease.*

I asked her, *How do you know how to get nervous?* She stopped and she said, *Well, I keep thinking I'm going to be nervous. Then the more I think I'm going to be nervous, the more I feel nervous and then I worry about it.* In order to worry, she had a worried voice in her head that talked to herself in a voice that stuttered and stammered which told her to look out and to be careful and not to make mistakes.

Whenever people are so worried about themselves rather than the feelings of other people, it's easy to get nervous. I told her instead to imagine being at that party and realizing that there were people all over that room that were more nervous than she was. I explained that her job was to find them and help them to feel comfortable because if she could make three other people feel comfortable and happy, her fears would disappear forever.

I remember she looked at me and said, *Really?* and I said, *Really*. Then, I told her the trick. *First, I want you to go back and remember the last time that you were at a party and you felt nervous and notice how the feelings spin inside your body. Literally freeze them, and reverse them and have them spin in the opposite direction. Then, look around the room and see who the most nervous person in the room looks like.* She said, *Me*.

I said, *Step inside yourself so that you can only see others. Look around the room. Pick the nervous person and then walk up and talk to them reassuringly, with jokes. Make them feel at ease and then move on to the next one and the next one.* We did this until she had gone through three people and was still feeling new feelings and spinning them in the reverse direction to her original feelings. The opposite of feeling nervous, of course, is being at ease. It's not being calm, it's about being at ease and really starting to be concerned with the well being of other people rather than being concerned about your own stomach.

The more you see, hear, and listen to other people while they talk and watch their expression and notice whether they're at ease, the more you can spend time doing things to make it so that they like you. The reason to do that is because the more they like you the more likely it is that they'll promote you. The more likely they are to invite you to another party. The more likely they are to introduce you to their friends. So it's important for you to do things that make them feel good. The more you focus on the outside and others out there, the less you'll focus on the inside.

Being at Ease with People

1. Think of a time when you are at a party or social gathering. Notice the feeling of nervousness and which way it is moving.
2. Imagine taking the feeling and reversing it so that it moves in the opposite direction. Spin it faster and faster in the opposite direction.
3. Become aware of the nervous voice inside your head and change it so that it says whatever it says in a very relaxed voice.
4. Move any images you have of you being rejected or looking nervous far away in the distance and, instead, replace them with images of the people that you talk to looking at you as you are feeling relaxed and at ease.
5. Imagine going from person to person, feeling at ease and making them feel good. Imagine making them smile and feel better about themselves and enjoying the whole event.

Meeting people is, of course, not just about going to parties. It is also about creating opportunities for relationships. It always surprises me how many people on this planet feel lonely and unhappy.

If you *are* desperately alone and unhappy, then maybe it's time you stopped worrying about it and started looking for one of those other six billion people out there who are feeling the very same as you. I meet so many people that claim that they want to meet somebody but they never go out and talk to anyone. These things are contradictory. You plan what you want. You plan how to get it. You think about it practically. If you don't make contact with lots of people, then it's going to be more difficult to find that one, right person.

When I taught flirting classes to people, I wasn't teaching them to go into bars and say, *Yo, baby*! I was explaining to them that if you don't meet a thousand people, then you don't have much of a selection. So you better get moving! Start walking up to people and talking to them. Some you won't want to talk to for thirty seconds. Some are good for an hour or two. One you might just want to spend your life with. If you don't meet enough people, you don't stand a chance of meeting *that* person. If you don't believe that it's possible, of course you won't try.

Tips on Flirting

1. When you see someone that you like smile at them.
2. Imagine yourself approaching them and feeling confident and at ease. See yourself speaking enticingly to them and then step into the movie.
3. Imagine two different scenarios. In the first, they reject you and you walk away confidently smiling and feeling glad that you didn't waste any time on them and that it's their loss. Imagine then scanning around you for someone else nice.
4. In the second, imagine them smiling back at you and accepting you and talking with you. Imagine making them smile and laugh and enjoying yourself with them.
5. Focus on making them feel really good around you rather than on having them like you. The better they feel around you, the more they will want to spend time with you.
6. Meet as many people as you can.

GETTING TO
Important Duties (Taxes and Study)

There are plenty of things that people need to do which they find difficult to motivate themselves to do. These important things, such as studying, doing taxes or doing the housework, are simple every day tasks that people often avoid because of procrastination.

Procrastination itself, by definition, is simply one of those things that people don't wait to do. People never wait to procrastinate. Again, we have another paradox. Since people don't wait to procrastinate, everybody reading this book can do some things immediately and can put others things off forever.

Some people put off taking a holiday forever. As I already mentioned, some put off telling their children that they love them. They wait until they are too grown. There are some things that aren't worth waiting for. Someone once asked me what the greatest difficulty in the human condition was. I said out of all the things that humans suffer from most, on the top of the list would be hesitation. My policy on hesitation is very simple. He who hesitates waits and waits and waits and waits, and the more you wait, the more you don't get it done. In order to end this cycle and get to the task in hand, we need to learn about how motivation works.

Understanding motivation starts out by looking at the difference between what people actually do and what they don't get around to. The difference between what they do and what they keep putting off and procrastinating about, or what they keep starting and not finishing, is that they are not propelled to getting it done. Once you have armed yourself with determination, it's a lot easier to get through things. But if you can get it so that you are moving towards things with excitement, it's a lot easier to get things done.

Some twenty-five years ago, a young man hired me because he had some sort of problem with his nose – it ran constantly. I put him into a hypnotic trance and I made him imagine he was in a desert and the running nose stopped. This turned out not to be the most important thing that I would help him with. The reason he was so concerned about it was because he was studying to become an opera singer.

He was a rather large man and had dreams of becoming like Pavarotti. He told me that his other problem was that, as much as he loved opera, he couldn't get himself to practice the amount he really needed to in order to become involved. He had a part in a local opera singing some things, but he never got leads. He never got parts because he simply never memorized the things he needed to be able to memorize.

Opera is a very complex task. I asked him at that point in time if there was anything that he easily motivated himself to do. He told me there was. It was cooking. He told me that he loved to cook gourmet meals and eat them. Looking at him, I could see that he did this on a fairly regular basis!

I asked him to stop and to think of himself sitting down to prepare himself a meal, cutting up all of the little things and doing all the seasoning. I asked him, even if he hadn't started it, if he thought about cooking that meal tonight, did he feel motivated?

He told me he did. I asked him how he knew that. His eyes drifted off, I could tell he had made an image in his mind and then he began to take his hand next to his body and he began to spin it in a forward motion. He told me he just becomes overwhelmed with a feeling.

We talked about spinning feelings. Spinning feelings isn't just something I made up, it is something I found. It is something that people do naturally. When people spin feelings faster and faster, of course their feelings get stronger and stronger, as long as they keep the ideas in their mind. When I asked him about studying this complex new opera that he was going to learn and asked him what happened he said, *Well I just struggle with it.*

Instinctively, his hand began to move in the opposite direction. Without him consciously understanding, he understood something that I have been using with people for years.

We were back at that stage again. It was time to take inventory. When I asked him to think about cooking the meals he looked in one place, when I asked him to think about opera he looked in another.

Again, the images were in different places. They were different sizes. One was a movie, one was a slide. One was in colour, one was in black and white. In one, he actually saw himself struggling studying the opera. In the other, he saw food and he saw himself eating it and being happy.

If you take the difference in all of the submodalities and different sensory systems and take the difference in the location, you can start to work with it. I made him take the opera and pull himself up so he saw himself happily studying the opera. I also had him spin the feelings of motivation faster and faster and then I added another element to it.

It's not enough to just snap an idea into place, you also have to have the appropriate steps. I also had him stop and think that he wanted to be this motivated. I had him take that image and look at it closely and then literally hold it up in his hand and look at it as if it was a photograph. Then let his other hand stand out and see him struggling the way he was now.

I got him to make a series of images, one leading to the next, leading to the next, and so on between one hand and the other so that he could see the logical step that would see him go from struggling, to see him being highly motivated and enjoying himself studying. In his case, it took sixteen different images.

Once they were all laid out between his hands and he could see all the steps from where he was to where he wanted to go, I had him push all of those images together inside of one image and pull it inside his body and spin the feeling of motivation faster and faster. So that not only did he have motivation, he had a plan. The difficulty most people have getting to things is that they have no plan.

Changing Your Feelings About Something (Visual Squash)

1. Think of something that you feel motivated to do. Notice the submodalities (A).
2. Think of something which makes you want to be motivated to do but you have struggled with. Notice the submodalities (B).
3. Take the image of what you want to be motivated to do (B) and send it off in the distance and back up into the position and submodalities of something you feel motivated to do (A).
4. Again, make an image of you struggling to do the activity or task in your mind and imagine it in your left hand. Imagine associating a colour and a shape with it. Make it a still image (C).
5. In your right hand, think of you completing it and feeling really good about it. Give that a colour and a shape. Make it a still image (D).
6. Crank up this positive, good feeling and imagine the colour and shape in your right hand getting bigger and stronger and more powerful. Turn up the feeling more and more until it's really intense.
7. Imagine between both hands are the different images of the different steps that need to be taken in order for you to go from the (C) image of you struggling to the (D) image of you enjoying the activity.
8. Take the image in the left hand and right hand and all the images in between and smack them together, filling the old feeling in the left hand with the positive feeling in the right hand so all of the images come together. Put your hands on your chest and imagine all of the feelings inside your body.

In order to get to things, you have to make decisions that you're going to do things quickly. We've already looked at an exercise to make good decisions. You might want to jump back to it and make a decision that you are going to do things sooner.

Take taxes for example. Like many of the things we are talking about, taxes are something that people hesitate to do and put off for as long as possible. Yet, if you can take the image of what produces intense desire in you, and you move the image of you doing taxes into that place, then you will start to feel like doing them. It really is that simple. You have an incredible ability inside your head to manifest the kinds of feelings that you need when you need them.

Getting to Your Taxes

1. Think of a big image of something that you absolutely love doing and just the thought of it makes you drool with desire. Notice the submodalities.
2. Imagine a small image of you doing your taxes in the centre of this image.
3. In a split second, imagine this small image growing into and replacing the bigger image so that you start to see yourself doing taxes in the same place and submodalities of what you drooled with desire for.
4. Repeat steps 1–3 a few times and notice yourself feeling the motivating feelings for when you think about doing your taxes.

The other thing about hesitation is that it functions as a bad habit. The trouble with bad habits is where people motivate themselves through anxiety. When I was in college, I was often amazed by how long people put off doing their term papers.

They would put off studying for tests until, with two weeks to the end of school, it would occur to them to start their term paper. They wouldn't have time to study for their finals and do everything but they kept going, *Well, I still got six weeks left. I've got five weeks left. I've got four weeks left. I've got three weeks left.*

Then, finally, with two weeks to go, they'd start to get nervous. With one week left, they'd have enough anxiety to motivate themselves to stay up all night typing away, trying to read books and trying to study for tests all at the same time.

I, on the other hand, decided to create my own stress. I would say, *Jeez, if I don't do everything in the first two weeks of school, I'll have to study for three months.* Instead, I did all my term papers right away. I read all the books and brought the books back to the bookstore as if I'd dropped a class and, as school went by, it made it easier for me.

The difference is, how do you define when to have your stress? If you're going to have it, you might as well do it sooner rather than later. Most people don't plan. Planning is everything. It's about looking into your timeline and deciding when to worry. If you must worry, you might as well do it sooner rather than later. It's even better to propel yourself by moving towards pleasure.

The more you can spin pleasure forward and make it so that you're drawn towards things, the easier it will be. It's as simple as seeing yourself doing something and then watching yourself do it happily, successfully and then stepping inside the picture so that you have the feelings. You can then spin them faster and faster and get on to it.

Getting to Study

1. Imagine something that you are really motivated to do and create the feeling and spin it inside you to intensify it.
2. Imagine yourself studying and doing really well in the exams.
3. Spin the feeling of motivation faster and faster as you think about studying and doing exams.
4. Think about not having enough time to study and spin the urgency.
5. Think about studying again and doing well in the exams as you spin the urgency and feeling of motivation faster and faster.

Over the years, I've had many very successful athletes who practiced things incessantly over and over again. None of them ever practiced because they were afraid of losing. They practiced because they loved the game. All of us love doing certain things rather than others. It's not the task itself that makes it good or bad. There are people that like adding columns of numbers.

I once had a client who was an accountant and he refused to use a computer because he loved doing numbers by hand. I always thought it as the slow way to do it but, for him, it was enjoyable because it was the thing he enjoyed doing. If people can enjoy adding numbers, and enjoy fishing off a boat, and love jumping out of aeroplanes, and enjoy playing golf, and enjoy all the silly things we do as human beings, then it's possible that you can make it so that you love anything.

GETTING TO

Exercise

Lots of people *want* to exercise but just don't do it. If you really want to do something, then you have to make it important. When you go through the submodalities in your mind, there are some things that are so important that you don't put them off. Somebody that claims to me that they have no discipline gets up every morning and showers and shaves. That's just contradictory to me. They have made it a part of their normal activity, and if they didn't do it something would feel *wrong*. The more they do it, the more right it feels.

You need to build propulsion systems, so that the more you don't do something, the more unpleasant it becomes, and the more you start to do it, the better it feels. A propulsion system simply means attaching powerfully positive feelings to doing something and attaching powerfully negative feelings to not doing something.

It has to begin at the right time. If your exercise equipment is in your garage, the feeling has to start from the moment you think about it to the moment you walk through the door until you climb on the machine. The closer you get to it the better it feels, the more you do it, the better you feel. The more you *don't* do it, the worse it feels. If you look at the treadmill and you don't walk up to it, it feels more unpleasant to walk away from it than to walk towards it.

You build an adequate propulsion system for everything – even if you have to go down to the gym. I lived with someone who, every day for a year, talked about going down to the gym, but never made it. He was a lunatic. I was in college and he would constantly talk about it. I finally bought him weights to have in the house and then he'd look at them and complain about how he didn't use them.

The truth is that he had his propulsion system backwards. The more he thought about the activity that he wanted to do, the worse he made himself feel. He would say, *I should do this but I'm not doing it* … back and forth and back and forth, rather than orchestrating it so that he was attracted to it. Getting control over which direction your feelings move is one of the best things about the submodality model.

You can change how you feel about something, so that instead of making it something you *should* do, it's something you really *desire*. One important step towards motivating yourself to do something is to change the words you use to yourself when talking about it. For example, as you already know, you don't always do what you *should* do but you might do what you *need to* do. These words are very powerful drivers for your behaviour. When you figure out which ones work best for you, you can begin to use those ones deliberately for when you need them. You will also learn to become aware of the tone and rhythm of your inner voice which most inspires and motivates you.

Motivate Yourself with Words

1. Think of something that you find yourself easily motivated to do.
2. Notice the tone of your inner voice and the rhythm of your inner voice that you use when you talk to yourself about these activities.
3. Become aware of the different words that work best to motivate you out of the following choices:

I WISH	I WANT	I NEED
I HAVE TO	I'VE GOT TO	I MUST
I SHOULD	I CAN	I WILL
I'M GOING TO	I AM DOING	

4. You will notice that some of these words work better for you than others and motivate you more than the others. Use the words and the tone and rhythm of the words and voice that motivates you.

Throughout this book, you've been given plenty of examples of how you can change your feelings towards something else. If you notice the submodalities of something you feel desire for and something you want to feel desire for, move what you want to feel desire for out into the distance and pull it back up in the submodalities of what you do desire. Then you will start to feel desire towards the new activity. This is called a swish pattern.

If you can use a swish pattern to build strong desires for any activity, the closer you get to that activity, the stronger your feelings get. The more you don't do it, the worse it gets. It will propel you in the right direction.

Most people try to get themselves to do things by feeling so bad that they finally do it. That doesn't work with doing things every day. People don't shave because they feel terrible. They shave because it's time to shave. They build a good habit, and they stick with it. It's not about creating great relief. It's about it feeling *right.* You make it so that something feels so good to do that it just feels right. That's why you just get up in the morning and you brush your teeth. If you walk out of the room and you realize that you haven't brushed your teeth, you just walk back in and do it. It becomes *second nature.*

The more you can make the things you want to do second nature, the easier they become. The more you make them a struggle, the more they will be. If you're struggling with any issue, whether it's jogging, or quitting smoking, or anything, the trick is to switch it in your mind first so that it becomes easier to do it. Most of the difficulties with the world that people have are not from the outside. I'm not saying that there aren't things on the outside that don't make things hard, I'm saying that most of the difficulty comes from the inside.

There really isn't anything between you and your exercise machine that's stopping you. There aren't two big thugs beating you every time you try to get on the exercise machine or do something. There are places in the world where such things go on, but most of us don't live in them. So, who's beating you up and stopping you from getting on the machine? It must be you!

You have to go inside and make it so that the more you think about it, the more you want it. You have to make it so the more you see yourself getting on the machine and being happier, and step inside that picture, the easier it's going to be.

How to Exercise Regularly

1. Think of a habit that you have and do every single day such as brushing your teeth or taking a shower. Notice the submodalities.
2. Think of exercising regularly. Notice the submodalities.
3. Think of how awful it will feel to be overweight, lazy and be feeling lethargic and unfit. Attach this to the thought of not exercising.
4. Think of how you will feel if you do exercise regularly and how good it will be to look great and feel great.
5. Take the image of you exercising and move it out and back into the image of you engaging in the habit that you do every day. Do this a few times quickly as you attach the good feeling. Do it until exercising feels like second nature to you.

GETTING TO
Be More Organized

Everybody wants to be more organized, however, most people don't organize themselves to be able to do it. They look at the chaos in their lives and they say to themselves, *I should do something about this*, and then they get a bad feeling and they avoid it. Therein lies the secret. The secret is that you have to go inside and take a small piece of the task and think about it differently.

If you look at a closet and it's piled high with junk, the first thing to know about how to use your mind is that in order to create order you must create more chaos. You must pull everything out of the closet. You must sort out the things that you're going to keep from the things you're not going to keep. Then you have to decide how you are going to put them back in so that they'll stay organized.

You have to do this, whether it's paperwork, whether it's clothes in the closet, whether it's shoes, whether it's your kitchen. You have to go in and be able to have a plan and then you have to go and create chaos so that you pull everything out. This means that you have to set aside time to do it. You have to set it up so that there are incremental tasks that you can actually accomplish. If you go and tear your closet apart and then you have to go to work and you come home and your whole house is upside down, it'll just make you crazy.

You have to do it in pieces and make sure that it fits in with your own life. You have to set aside time and then decide at the end that it is going to feel wonderful and make every day easier. Then you have to look at yourself living in that universe where your closet stays clean and where you put your shoes back where they belong and see what it looks like.

You have to see whatever kind of order that you want to create in your life. Then you have to back up and decide, *In order to get to that place, I have to create this much chaos and it's going to take this much time*, so that you see yourself going through the chaos. If you don't think that you look like you're enjoying the process of pulling everything out because you're thinking about the fact that you could be playing tennis or going to the beach then, of course, you're going to suffer.

However, if you look at it in steps so that you break it into pieces – you have a piece that you can accomplish and you make sure that the closer you get to the end of it the better you feel – then it will be different. The first thing is that you have to pull everything out and then sort everything out and then you have to have a plan for how you are going to put it back in. It's not good enough to pull everything out of your garage and not know what you're going to do with it. If you don't mentally plan, then you're not mentally organized. If you're not mentally organized, then it's harder to create organization on the outside.

This is also why some people are too organized. You have some people who end up being clean freaks to the point that if one fork is out of place, they go ballistic. They over-plan things. Whenever you over-plan or under-plan you haven't really got a useful plan, so what you need to do is to be able to create a realistic plan. It is a plan that also involves you looking happy and being happy.

The trick is that you look at it so much that you desire it. You move it into the submodalities of your strongest desire so that you feel drawn towards doing it. You make sure every single piece of the plan fits within your schedule and you'll feel good when it's done.

Your plan should also have a way to keep it that way so that you don't end up redoing big things over and over again. Instead, it takes care of itself. You can wait until your car is completely dirty or you could wash it on a semi-regular basis, given that you don't drive it through the mud like a four-wheel drive vehicle. However, if you drive it through the mud, you should go and spray it off before the mud hardens, just like you do with yourself.

You don't wait till you're stinking or horribly dirty before you wash. You take a shower or bath on a regular basis. You get up and you clean yourself off and you brush your teeth. It's not a struggle. It becomes a good habit. If you plan to have good habits, you will and if you don't, you won't.

If you believe it's going to be hard, then it will be and if you believe it's just the natural order of life, then it'll be easy. I recommend that you make things easier rather than planning on making them difficult because if you plan on them being difficult, they will be. If you plan on them and believe in them being easy, they get easier.

Getting To Be More Organized

1. Take whatever area in your life that you would like to be more organized and think of how exactly you would like to organize things. Set yourself enough time for the task.

2. Imagine yourself taking everything out and looking at everything and sorting things out into different chunks and sections. Imagine yourself sorting them out and placing them back in an organized system. See yourself enjoying the process.

3. Take everything apart and out and then begin to fit things into different categories that you have set up. Next, start putting everything back in a new order.

4. Set up a discipline whereby you continuously keep things in order and monitor yourself on a regular basis.

GETTING TO
Make More Money

Everybody tells me they want to make more money. Even the richest people I've ever met want to make more money. There are no easy answers to this because it depends on where you are and what you're doing. The one rule that I'm sure of is that if you get paid by the hour, then the only way to get paid more is to work more hours.

You have to find some way of taking your own resources and investing them in some way. Some people invest in the stock market, but it's best that you know about the stock market and play it on paper before you sink real money into it. Some people buy an old house and fix it up – I used to do this. I would buy old, cheap properties and then renovate them and add a room, paint them, landscape the gardens, then sell them on at a profit. Given that I had friends who were contractors and I understood the process, it was possible to make money at it. But you could also lose money doing this.

The big mistake that people, even billionaires, are guilty of is that they make their fortune excelling at one business and then somebody comes along and tells them about another opportunity – one in which they have no experience – and they leap in. Rather than acting on their long personal history of what makes sense in their area of expertise and making good decisions, they trust somebody else. The problem is that when they do this, they have no basis on which to decide if something is the right choice or not. They risk losing a lot of money.

I have a friend who owns ten car lots and knows all there is to know about the automobile industry. Somebody came along and advised him to invest in a different area. He sought my advice claiming, *I could make millions on this!* I replied, *Yeah, but you can make millions doing what you're doing. Why not take your money and invest in twenty car lots, because you'll know what you're doing, as opposed to investing in something that you know nothing about.* This isn't just true for billionaires, it is true for all of us.

I'm a very entrepreneurial person and I think that even if a person has a job, they should have some small business on the side. Especially with the Internet nowadays, which opens up a world of opportunity for people to have a small business. Make one little thing and start to sell it on the side, or one service – something you can grow into a business of your own – so that you're not simply working by the hour. Pretty soon, you can have other people working by the hour. That's a good thing.

There are two kinds of income. There's generative income and time-based income. A lot of people work at a job and eventually get a raise and then another raise. If you're in the right profession, eventually you can do fairly well. But if you're in the wrong one, you can spend your whole life working, doing the same thing, because you don't have the belief that you can nurture a little acorn into a massive oak.

On this planet, especially in free societies, opportunity abounds everywhere. It really does. The only thing that stops most people is a lack of belief that they can do something simple. They don't have to give up what they're doing. They just have to start something.

If you build the right beliefs and look at things through the correct lens, and if you plan well, and don't do things that you don't understand just because someone else tells you it's a winner, you can succeed in enterprise. You need to make sure you talk to people who have actually done it.

It was such a surprise to me that you could go to people who had successfully run businesses from their teens to their retirement and you could sit down and ask them about it and they would tell you everything you wanted to know. The reason that they did it for all those years wasn't that they made money at it, it was because they loved it. I got people who were heads of big corporations to tell me about business and to advise me on potential mistakes, pitfalls, and oversights.

Most people who start firms aren't smart enough, they often put their accountant or their lawyer on their board of directors, and that's a big mistake. Instead, find people who have succeeded and let them be your advisors. The reason they did what they did is that they were good at it. You can't expect someone – a lawyer or an accountant – who has never succeeded in commerce to be able to give sound advice. A board of directors is supposed to direct you in how to succeed. You should find people that you don't know, that have no emotional attachment to you, or vested interest in anything bar the success of the business. If you're the one with the expertise, it might not make sense to do things exactly the way they say. You should be the one making the decisions, and when you don't have the expertise, find people who do.

The planet is full of millionaires. When I was young, there really weren't that many around. There are currently throngs of highly successful people walking our streets. There are also many very successful retired people who would be glad to share the secrets of their past successes.

There are always people at banks who can give you advice about how to bank more intelligently. However, they can't really give you good advice about what to do with the money you borrow from them, otherwise they wouldn't be working in a bank. They can only tell you about banking – people can only tell you about what they know. If you keep that in mind, and if you talk to enough people, and you get enough sensible advice, you can progress. But if you sit at home and moan, *I can never do this. Nothing's gonna happen,* then you'll be right.

I recommend that you be wrong about this. Go out and find out about what you don't know, learn it, and spend a lot of time doing it. I know so many people that started with nothing and now have a whole lot of something. I recommend you become one of them.

How to Make More Money

1. Build a belief in yourself being wealthy.
2. You can do this by going back to the Inventory where you found the submodalities of a strong belief. Take the thought of you becoming successfully wealthy in the near future and move it off and back up into the submodalities of the strong belief. Do this a number of times.
3. Focus on making your money based upon what you know rather than something you don't know much about.
4. Learn everything that you need to know about whatever business or opportunity that you are looking at. Research in depth so that you are absolutely clear on everything.
5. Find a mentor who has already succeeded in the business that you are in and ask them all the questions you have about how to make it work.
6. Always ask how you can be more valuable to the world and prepare to work more effectively than ever before.

GETTING TO
Make Big Decisions

Making humungous decisions, like what you're going to do for the rest of your life, are a challenge for some people. They come to me and they say, *I need to decide what I'm going to do for the rest of my life!* I always start out by asking, *What do you want to do tomorrow?* They always look at me blankly and say something like, *Well, I have to go to work tomorrow …* I say, *I didn't say that; I said what do you want to do tomorrow? Even if you only have an hour off between work and another job, what are you going to do with the free time? If you can't figure out how to be happy for an hour, how are you going to manage it for the rest of your life?*

People are always telling me that they want to win the lottery because if they had millions of dollars, they would be happy. However, I have lots of exceptionally rich clients who are quite miserable. Money doesn't necessarily make you happy. If you can't be

166

happy with a thousand dollars, how are you going to be happy with a million?

People somehow believe that things are easier when you're rich, but maybe the opposite is true – with unlimited money, you have to make more decisions about what you're going to do and how you're going to keep it and how you're going to spend it. You have to be able to decide who to trust and who not to trust.

Other people might say, *I want to travel the world!* First, shouldn't you be able to take short trips and enjoy them? If you leave your house and you go to India, you're not necessarily going to be more satisfied there if you hate unfamiliarity or you don't know what to do. Travelling is a skill, like anything else. You should take it in small steps, get really good at it, and then take bigger steps.

You don't have to commit yourself to travel for fifteen years, take a trip for two weeks and, if you enjoy that, next time go for a month. Make plans for how you're actually going to enjoy yourself when you're there. They don't need to come from a travel agent, they come from seeing yourself in those situations. You've seen enough television and movies, and you've spoken to enough people to find out what to do.

If you just send yourself off to a foreign country, and do all the touristy things, you won't necessarily enjoy yourself. Some people enjoy travelling on buses because they get to talk to people, while some people hate buses. You have to decide what it is you enjoy doing. Once you know what you enjoy, you can plan how to get there and do it.

You need to be able to fantasize. When people are picking out careers, for example, it amazes me that they never go to watch people doing that job. I ask people in medical school if they have ever hung around a hospital and all they can say is, *Why?* I say, *Because you want to be a doctor! Even before you go into private practice, you're going to have to spend years as a resident, and you might end up working in a hospital. Wouldn't it be nice to know if what goes on there is actually something that you want to do?* If you're becoming a doctor so that you can be rich, why bother? There are loads of other, less stressful ways to get rich.

Deciding that something you get is going to make you happy is doomed to fail. If you're going to do something for the rest of your life, it had better be something that you really enjoy, not just something that allows you two weeks a year to do something that you actually enjoy.

When weighing good decisions and bad decisions, don't view them as slides or a bunch of still images, see them as very long movies, day by day. If you're going to have a job, you're going to have to get up in the morning and do it all day long. If it isn't something that you might at least potentially enjoy, you're in trouble. There should be multiple benefits to your job, not just one but a lot of them.

I find that people sell themselves too short and the reason that they never get around to things is that they don't have at least five really good choices, and their choices aren't based on enough experience. You need to talk to people who actually do these things and find out what they do every day. People are going to take trips but they need to know what goes on when they get there.

The first time I took a holiday on my own, I went to Mexico. On the way down there, I was with a fairly wealthy couple and we were driving in a convoy of fourteen cars. All the lady talked about on the way down was about how she was going to buy blankets in Mexico. By the time we got there, I was completely fixated on buying a blanket because I thought that that's what you went to Mexico to do. When I got down there, there were all kinds of lovely things going on. I eventually left the convoy because they were obsessed with buying artifacts from the locals, statues, and weird hats. These were things I didn't need. I found out there was a whole world of things I could do down there and enjoy.

My favourite thing was just talking to the people. Even if they didn't speak English, I liked listening to them. My Spanish wasn't that good, but by the time I got back, it was better. If you really listen to people, it's easy to understand them, especially English and Spanish, they're very similar languages. 'Atencion' in Spanish and 'Attention' in English, are closely related. If you really listen to people and you watch what they're doing, and you pay attention to what they enjoy when they're there, it gives you much better choices about what you can do.

One day on that holiday, I was on the lake and there was a guy fishing. I watched him fish for a while and then I went and did the same. I caught a few trout. I'd never been fishing before, I was a city boy. The only water supply we had was the bay, and there were signs everywhere warning against fishing because the fish were lethal because of the mercury levels! That's back when we used to pour sewage into our water supply. When I was young, the belief was that you couldn't actually pollute water, that the sewage would somehow mysteriously disappear – we know better now. The idea of not putting sewage into what you drink is a good idea *mentally*.

When making big plans that will have repercussions for years, take it a piece at a time. Be able to see yourself in those situations. Imagine what's going to happen. When you get there, there will always be things better than what you had imagined, and that's a good thing. There may be a few things that might be worse too, those will be the things to avoid.

Making Life Decisions

1. Think about the decision you have to make. Find out the submodalities and whether it fits into the good or bad decision submodalities that you elicited earlier in this book.
2. Imagine the different potential outcomes from each decision. Run a movie right out into the future, seeing all of the impact and effects of each decision on your entire life.
3. Look back through each of the movies of each decision and decide on the decision that works the best for you.
4. Take into account any negative consequences as a result of making that decision and decide how you are going to deal with them.

Tips for Going Travelling

1. Decide where you want to go and for what kind of trip. Ask yourself why you want to go.
2. Research all the information you will need for the holiday. How to get there. What you will need to bring. What you need to do when you get there. Further travel arrangements. Where you are going to stay.
3. Make sure you take into account what you need to get done before you go away and what systems you need to put in place so your work can cope when you're gone so that you can fully enjoy your trip away.
4. Get lots of new experiences and meet as many people as you can.

You will start to find that, once you build motivation, you will become drawn towards things that you want to or need to do. The more you manifest hope and excitement about the future, the more you have to look forward to. And the more you have to look forward to, the easier it is for you to organize your perceptions, feelings and even your life. The future is full of opportunities and the more you get to those things that make your life better, the more you'll discover that there are more good times ahead of you than you could possibly imagine.

CONCLUSION

Looking back on what you've read so far, what I have presented here is a variety of ways of organizing your internal world so that you have more control over what your brain does. It's essential that you have more control over how you feel and so more control over what you do. If you change the way you think, it changes the way you feel, which changes the way you act.

When I started out nearly four decades ago, people were looking at things from a psychological point of view. They wanted to know why you had problems and that if they knew the source of the problems, they'd mysteriously change somehow. The behavioural technology that I created was made out of discovering how people did things successfully, how they got over things, how they got through things, how they got to things and what it is that it takes for humans to live more efficiently.

The lessons that I have presented in this book are nothing more than lessons in how to manage life. They are lessons in how to manage your thoughts, your feelings and your time, so that life becomes more wonderful. This isn't a philosophy. This isn't an ideology. It's not a religion. It is just a set of tools to make things easier. The easier you can make it inside your head, the easier it will make things outside your head. It will not only be easier for you but for those around you. It will allow you to live more happily.

All the patterns that are used inside this book of the kind of work that I do will have no value if you don't get around to using them. Once you get over a fear of elevators, it's not enough. You have to get around to getting into an elevator until you're sure. If you wait too long, it just won't work. You may not be afraid but if you don't do it, then your life doesn't have the freedom that you want. It's about achieving this freedom so that you can control your life.

Your brain runs all the time, and it's either going to run in the direction you want it to go or it's going to run all over the place. If you don't do things to control your thoughts and to control what pictures you make, then you won't be feeling as good as you can be feeling. It's important to organize and manage your thoughts, your time and even manage your sleep so that when you lay down at night you tell yourself that you're going to sleep easily. I know people that spend hours telling themselves that they won't get to sleep when it's the process of talking too much that keeps them awake!

The more you learn to put volume controls on your internal voices and to place pictures methodically, to choose what you're going to believe and what you're not going to believe, the more you're in charge of your own mental processes, the more you'll be in charge of your life.

Conclusion

Get the Life You Want is simply this: my suggestions to you to control yourself, in a good way, not in a way that you're so controlled that you can't do what you want, but in a way where you *aim* your life. If you aim your thoughts and you aim your feelings and you aim your conscious and your unconscious desires in the same direction, there's literally nothing that humans can't accomplish.

When I was born, people used to compare something that was impossible with putting a man on the moon. Yet, in a short space of time – within fifteen years of my birth – there was a man on the moon looking down at the earth and saying that it was a *Giant leap for mankind*.

The truth is that out of the space project came all kinds of by-products; one of those was disposable hypodermic needles. It is responsible for wiping smallpox off the face of the earth. When we set great tasks in front of us and we put all our resources towards them, the by-products can often be wonderful things.

The same thing is true of your own life. When you make great, big goals – whether you get to them or not – the things that happen along the way are what makes life wonderful. The people that you meet, the things that you accomplish, the more you don't waste time going in circles and fighting with yourself, the more you'll get to do things and try things. Some of those things are going to work out wonderfully. I hope that what you've learned here makes your life easier.

If it does, drop me a note. I like all the good feedback I can get! Thank you very much.

Richard Bandler

POSTSCRIPT
From the editor

I am very excited to write this postscript to Richard Bandler's *Get the Life You Want*. Over the past thirty-five years, Richard Bandler has been teaching workshops to people all over the world, helping them to discover the secrets behind the magical process of personal change. In this book, he continues to share his ideas with the world in ways which are so simple in their approach.

Speaking as a psychologist, the more time goes by, the more we realize that the latest findings and research in the Psychology of Change are only just catching up with Richard's ideas. We are only now beginning to accept that change can take place quickly and more easily than we considered before.

In the early 1970s, Richard Bandler co-created the field of NLP, or Neuro-Linguistic Programming, with John Grinder. Since then, Richard has continued to evolve his ideas beyond what was considered possible and, today, his work is taught in educational systems, universities, hospitals, and businesses across the globe. NLP has revolutionized our understanding of human beings and what it is possible for us to accomplish by mastering our own minds.

In his own, unique style, Richard targets the main areas of personal change and offers technique after technique that you can use to ensure that you achieve lasting change. This is by far one of the most practical books Richard has ever written and is a wonderful way of bringing his insights into transformation to the world. While experienced NLP students will learn greatly from it, its true power lies in its simplicity and the fact that it gives you things you can immediately practice and do, for long lasting results.

While there are thousands of speakers out there in the field of personal change, Richard stands head and shoulders above all of them. His ability to help people to change is unparalleled, as is his unique sense of humour and creative genius.

What lies inside these pages are the techniques that Richard has used over the past thirty-five years with his clients to help them overcome their problems and get the kind of life they want. From getting over things and getting through things to getting to them, Richard presents a guide that everyone should carry with them.

Having worked with thousands of people from all over the world with different kinds of problems, I have found that people's biggest barriers to change are often their own minds and, more specifically, their own beliefs. We have been trained to believe that change isn't easy and requires a lot of effort and a lot of time. I've always found this to be simply not true.

Sometimes, people hang on to their problems because they want to feel unique or important. Their problems give them an identity.

They love to be a *victim* of the world. They seek out to prove that nothing will work for them and that they are hopeless cases. Over the years, if there's one thing I've learned from Richard, and experienced in my own life, it is that there is no such thing as a hopeless case. There is always hope and there is always a way out of your problems. You can take control over your beliefs and you can stop getting in your own way. You can believe in your ability to get over things, through things, and to them. You can also discover that the process of change is actually far simpler than you think.

Something else that holds people back is that they think about their problems as their permanent state of being. They worry that any change will 'wear off'. Of course, nothing could be further from the truth. In reality, we learn limiting and non-useful behaviours in terms of our thoughts as well as our actions. The good news is that it is possible for you to enjoy freedom from these problems. Nothing 'wears off' because as long as you think differently, you will feel differently.

Get the Life You Want is not a long list of elaborate theories on why things in life are messed up. Nor is it a list of reasons about why change is difficult. Instead, in the pages, there are techniques which you can immediately use to overcome your problems and begin to do what it is that you want with your life. At long last, from Richard Bandler himself, the co-creator of one of the most important and successful personal development models of all time, there is a book which tells you what to do.

Many people have written books on NLP, coaching and presented techniques from NLP – and much of what has been written in these books is based on Richard's ideas. In this book, you get the real skills and techniques from the original creative genius himself. In Richard's stories and the examples he gives from his work with clients, you will also get an insight into how he approaches problems and you will find his attitude of determination, perseverance and his super sense of humour, so contagious in its impact on you.

In order for you to get the best from this book, study the inventory closely and use the techniques outlined by Richard – try them all out. You will find yourself able to overcome all the problems that are contained within this book. Furthermore, it will help you begin a journey towards making your life as wonderful as it can be.

In my experience, the biggest challenge people face is learning to get out of their own way. When you can see just how easy change can be, you can begin to take control over your life and make all the changes that you want. But you need to take the action. It is so important that you follow through on these exercises and techniques. If you do, you will get the result. If you don't, you won't. It's that simple.

It reminds me of the tale of the King and the Boulder. Once upon a time, there was a king who placed a huge boulder on a roadway. Then he hid himself and watched to see if anyone would remove the huge rock. Some of the king's wealthiest merchants and courtiers came by and simply walked around it. Many blamed the king loudly for not keeping the roads clear, but none did anything about getting the stone out of the way.

Then a peasant came along carrying a load of vegetables. Upon approaching the boulder, the peasant laid down his burden and tried to move the stone to the side of the road. After much pushing and straining, he finally succeeded.

Postscript

After the peasant picked up his load of vegetables, he noticed a purse lying in the road where the boulder had been. The purse contained many gold coins and a note from the king saying that the gold was for the person who removed the boulder from the road.

We all have choices of how to deal with the boulders in our life. This book is your opportunity to learn how to move them out of your way and find the treasure that lies in your future of freedom.

Owen Fitzpatrick
presenter of RTE1's *Not Enough Hours*
and co-founder of the Irish Institute of NLP

GLOSSARY OF TERMS

Below is a list of some of the main processes related to NLP that are discussed in this book.

Auditory
Relating to the sense of hearing.

Behaviour
The specific actions we take.

Conscious Mind
The part of your mind that is working when you are alert and aware. It is your critical faculty and your source of reason and logic. It seems to run constantly all day while you are awake and its focus is always on particular thoughts. It is mainly controlled by the automatic processes of the unconscious mind.

Criteria

The values a person uses to make decisions.

Design Human Engineering

A technology and evolutionary tool created by Richard Bandler in the late 1980s–early 1990s which focuses on using more of our brain to do more than was previously possible.

Gustatory

Relating to the sense of taste.

Hypnosis

An application of NLP as well as a field in its own right. Hypnosis is the process of guiding a person into a state where they have more direct access to their unconscious mind, which is where powerful changes can be made, deliberately through the use of suggestion.

Kinesthetic

Related to body sensations.

Meta Model

A model developed by Richard Bandler and John Grinder that suggests questions that enable people to specify information, clarify information, and open up and enrich the model of a person's world.

Meta Program

A learned process for sorting and organizing information and internal strategies.

Milton Model

A model developed by Richard Bandler and John Grinder on the patterns of hypnotic techniques used by Milton H. Erickson, the clinical hypnotherapist, and other masters of persuasion.

Neuro-Hypnotic Repatterning

Using Hypnosis to make changes in people on a neurological level so that they can change how they feel about something.

Neuro-Linguistic Programming

An attitude, methodology, and technology that teaches people how to improve the quality of their lives. It is an educational tool that teaches people how to communicate more effectively with themselves and with others. It is designed to help people to have personal freedom in the way they think, feel, and behave.

Representational Systems

The five systems that we take information in from the world. Through these systems (our five senses) we create a representation of the information we take in.

State

The total ongoing mental, emotional, and physical conditions of a person at a given moment of time.

Strategy

A set of mental and behavioural steps to achieve an outcome.

Submodalities

We represent the world internally through five senses. We take the information in through our senses and then make internal images, sounds, feelings, tastes and smells. Once we do this, the way in which we represent our experiences through these five internal senses will often determine how we feel about them. So, how big the images you make of spiders might effect how scared you are of them. The tone of your internal voice might determine if you are bored or not. The qualities of these internal representations are known as Submodalities.

Timelines

The way that we code time internally. Our images of the past, present, and future are represented somewhere in our immediate space. Some people represent their past in front of them and to their left, the present straight in front of them, and their future in front of them and to their right. This is known as through time. Other people represent the future in front of them and the past behind them. This is known as *in* time. Many people have a mixture of both of these patterns.

Trance

A state commonly experienced as a result of hypnosis. It is also a state of mind that is characterized by a focus of thought. We live in many different trances depending on what our mind is absorbed in at any given moment (television, driving, eating, etc).

Unconscious Installation

The process of installing skills, ideas, and suggestions inside a person through communicating with their unconscious mind.

Unconscious Mind

The part of your mind that is working all the time. It is what produces your dreams and regulates your bodily functions such as your heartbeat, breathing, and habitual patterns of behaviour. It contains all your memories, wisdom, and perception. It runs the automatic programs of thinking and behaving and therefore is the best place to make changes permanent.

Well-Formed Outcomes

Goals that are set according to well-formed conditions. These conditions are that the goals must be positive, specific, sensory based, ecological, and maintainable by the individual.

Visual

Relating to the sense of sight.

RECOMMENDED RESOURCES

Books

Bandler, Richard & Owen Fitzpatrick, *Conversations: 'Freedom is Everything and Love is all the Rest'* (Mysterious Publishing, 2005).

Bandler, Richard & John Grinder, *The Structure of Magic, Volume 1* (Meta Publications, 1975).

Bandler, Richard & John Grinder, *The Structure of Magic, Volume 2* (Meta Publications, 1975).

Bandler, Richard & John Grinder, *Patterns of the Hypnotic Techniques of Milton H. Erickson, Volume 1* (Meta Publications, 1975).

Bandler, Richard, Judith Delozier & John Grinder, *Patterns of the Hypnotic Techniques of Milton H. Erickson, Volume 2* (Meta Publications, 1977).

Bandler, Richard & John Grinder, *Trance-formations* (Real People Press, 1980).

Bandler, Richard & John Grinder, *Frogs Into Princes* (Real People Press, 1979).

Bandler, Richard & John LaValle, *Persuasion Engineering* (Meta Publications, 1996).

Bandler, Richard & Will McDonald, *An Insider's Guide to Submodalities* (Meta Publications, 1989).

Bandler, Richard, *Magic in Action* (Meta Publications, 1985).

Bandler, Richard, *The Adventures of Anybody* (Meta Publications, 1993).

Bandler, Richard, *Time for a Change* (Meta Publications, 1993).

Bandler, Richard, *Using Your Brain for a Change* (Real People Press, 1985).

McKenna, Paul, *Change your Life in Seven Days* (Bantam, 2005).

Wilson, Robert Anton, *Prometheus Rising* (New Falcon Press, 1983).

Wilson, Robert Anton, *Quantum Psychology* (New Falcon Press, 1990).

DVD and CD Products

Bandler, Richard, *Persuasion Engineering* (DVD).

Bandler, Richard, *The Art and Science of Nested Loops* (DVD).

Bandler, Richard, *DHE 2000* (CD).

Bandler, Richard, *Personal Enhancement Series* (CD).

LaValle, John, *NLP Practitioner Set* (CD).

These and many more DVDs and CDs are both hypnotic and from seminars Richard does.

Available from www.nlpstore.com

Adventures in Neuro-Hypnotic Repatterning (DVD set and PAL-
  version videos).
Thirty Years of NLP: How to Live a Happy Life (DVD set) and
  other products by Richard Bandler.

Available from Matrix Essential Training Alliance

www.meta-nlp.co.uk; email: enquiries@meta-nlp.co.uk
tel +44 (0)1749 871126; fax +44 (0)1749 870714

Websites

http://www.richardbandler.com
http://www.NLPInstitutes.com
http://www.NLPTrainers.com
http://www.NLPLinks.com
http://www.purenlp.com
http://www.paulmckenna.com
http://www.neuroing.com
http://www.meta-nlp.co.uk
http://www.rawilson.com

The Society of Neuro-Linguistic Programming™

Richard Bandler Licensing Agreement

The Society of Neuro-Linguistic Programming™ is set up for the purpose of exerting quality control over those training programmes, services and materials claiming to represent the model of Neuro-Linguistic Programming™ (NLP™). The seal below indicates Society Certification and is usually advertised by Society approved trainers. When you purchase NLP™ products and seminars, ask to see this seal. This is your guarantee of quality.

It is a common experience for many people when they are introduced to NLP™ and first begin to learn the technology to be cautious and concerned with the possible uses and misuses.

As a protection for you and for those around you, the Society of NLP™ now requires participants to sign a licensing agreement which guarantees that those certified in this technology will use it with the highest integrity. It is also a way to ensure that all the training you attend is of the highest quality and that your trainers are updated and current with the constant evolution of the field of Neuro-Linguistic Programming™ and Design Human Engineering™, etc.

For a list of recommendations, go to:

http://www.NLPInstitutes.com,
http://www.NLPTrainers.com
http://www.NLPLinks.com.

The Society of NLP
NLP™ Seminars Group International
PO Box 424
Hopatcong
NJ 07843
USA

Tel: 00 1 (973) 770 3600
Website: www.purenlp.com

© 1994 The Society of NLP™ and Richard Bandler.